Supporting Stu[dents]
on th[e]
Autism Spe[ctrum]

Supporting Students on the Autism Spectrum

A Practical Guide for Academic Libraries

Rachel M. McMullin and Kerry R. Walton

LIBRARIES UNLIMITED™

An Imprint of ABC-CLIO, LLC

Santa Barbara, California • Denver, Colorado

Library of Congress Cataloging-in-Publication Data

Names: McMullin, Rachel M., author. | Walton, Kerry R., author.
Title: Supporting students on the autism spectrum : a practical guide for academic libraries / Rachel M. McMullin and Kerry R. Walton.
Description: Santa Barbara : Libraries Unlimited, [2019] | Includes bibliographical references and index.
Identifiers: LCCN 2018059561 (print) | LCCN 2019010073 (ebook) | ISBN 9781440863974 (ebook) | ISBN 9781440863967 (pbk. : alk. paper)
Subjects: LCSH: Libraries and the developmentally disabled. | Academic libraries—Services to people with disabilities. | Autism spectrum disorders.
Classification: LCC Z711.92.D48 (ebook) | LCC Z711.92.D48 M37 2019 (print) | DDC 027.6/63—dc23
LC record available at https://lccn.loc.gov/2018059561

ISBN: 978-1-4408-6396-7 (paperback)
        978-1-4408-6397-4 (ebook)

23 22 21 20 19   1 2 3 4 5

This book is also available as an eBook.

Libraries Unlimited
An Imprint of ABC-CLIO, LLC

ABC-CLIO, LLC
147 Castilian Drive
Santa Barbara, California 93117
www.abc-clio.com

This book is printed on acid-free paper ∞

Manufactured in the United States of America

This book discusses treatments (including types of medication and mental health therapies), diagnostic tests for various symptoms and mental health disorders, and organizations. The authors have made every effort to present accurate and up-to-date information. However, the information in this book is not intended to recommend or endorse particular treatments or organizations, or substitute for the care or medical advice of a qualified health professional, or used to alter any medical therapy without a medical doctor's advice. Specific situations may require specific therapeutic approaches not included in this book. For those reasons, we recommend that readers follow the advice of qualified health-care professionals directly involved in their care. Readers who suspect they may have specific medical problems should consult a physician about any suggestions made in this book.

Contents

Acknowledgments

We are beyond grateful for some very important and special people who have supported us from the start of an exciting idea through the completion of this book.

To Cherie Fishbaugh and the students and graduate assistants in West Chester University's DCAP program—your time, your excitement, and most importantly, your own experiences and words have helped shape this book. It would not be the same without you, and we are extremely grateful for our strong relationship. We have learned so much from all of you, and you have made us better librarians.

To our editor, Jessica Gribble—without meeting you at ACRL 2016 and your saying, "I think this can be a book," this would not be a book. Thank you for believing in the topic and us and your support along the way.

To our library deans—Mary Page and Amy Ward—your unwavering support and encouragement kept us going, especially when we landed in your office frazzled, whiney, or grumpy.

To our colleagues who also showed constant support and encouragement and didn't bat an eye when we ate our stress in donuts.

Finally, and most importantly, to our families:

To our husbands and kiddoes—your patience, understanding, and love mean the world to us. We could not have done this without your laughter and smiles and lots of eating out!

Introduction

STUDENTS WITH ASD ARE HERE

If you have not yet worked with students with autism spectrum disorder (ASD) in your academic library, you will be soon. The prevalence rate of ASD has risen dramatically from 1 to 150 in 2000, to 1 in 88 in 2008, and most recently to 1 in 59 in 2018 (Centers for Disease Control and Prevention, n.d.). The statistics for 2008 (1 in 88) were based on children born in 2000, a group that is now college aged. Many of these individuals are of average or above average intelligence, and with support have been very successful in their primary and secondary education. The next logical step for them, as with any successful graduating senior, is to attend college. In fact, many are already attending college, as shown in a 2011 study of current college students at a large public university. The study found the rate of ASD among students ranging from .7 to 1.9 percent (from 1 in 130 to 1 in 53) students (White, Ollendick, and Bray 2011). That is very much in line with the figures for the general population. Elementary, middle, and high school education practices have all changed and adapted to meet the needs of this population, and now colleges and universities need to do the same.

WHY THIS BOOK?

Making libraries accessible and meeting the needs of diverse populations are topics of importance to all librarians, including academic librarians. This is reflected in several policies published by the American Library Association and its divisions (ACRL 2012; ALA 2009; ASCLA 2006) and in the body of recent library science research (Cooke 2016; Hernon and Calvert 2006; Small, Myhill, and Herring-Harrington 2015). However, because college students with ASD are a group that is only emerging now in significant numbers, there is very little research specific to them and their experience with academic libraries. Although there is a somewhat larger body of research related to working with autistic students and patrons in school and public library settings, it does not transfer well, due to difference in both the types of library services provided and the age and needs of college students. On the other hand, the general body of research on ASD is overwhelmingly vast, and the scholarship dedicated to the transition and success of students in college is growing very rapidly. It is difficult to sift through all that research to find sources that address the specific needs and concerns of academic libraries. This book is meant to fill that gap by presenting the results of the most recent research in a way that is tailored to the needs of academic librarians and staff and using a language they will understand. We have read all of the most recent research and pulled out the information that relates to academic libraries as well as all the best strategies and tips for working with students with ASD to present here. We have not attempted to be completely comprehensive in our review of the literature—the body of research is simply too large. Instead we have focused on research published in the last 10 years, going back farther than that only to tap classic works or to address a gap in the more current research.

MAKING STUDENTS WITH ASD FEEL WELCOME

A major predictor of whether students, including those with disabilities, remain at a particular college is the feeling of a sense of belonging (Fleming et al. 2017; O'Keeffe 2013). This sense of belonging depends on many factors including relationships with faculty and other students, overall campus climate, and engagement in activities on campus. As we will discuss more in Chapter 1, one of the major diagnostic criteria of ASD is deficits with social communication and interaction (DSM-5 2013), which can make it even more difficult for students on the spectrum to find their place on campus and achieve that sense of belonging. If librarians and library staff can make our academic libraries welcoming for students on the spectrum, and provide them with a space where they feel understood and valued, then we are making a significant contribution to their success. The first step in doing this is to encourage awareness and understanding of these students among librarians, library staff, and library administrators. The needs of students with ASD are unique and often quite distinct from other diverse populations on campus.

TERMINOLOGY

There is quite a bit of specialized terminology related to ASD. We have tried to be both thoughtful and consistent in what we have selected to use.

Autistic Person versus Person with Autism/ASD

The best language to use is deeply contested, as reflected in a recent study by Kenny et al. (2016). A majority of scholars and professionals who work with the population strongly prefer person-first language, such as *person with autism* or *person with ASD* rather than *autistic person*. This approach began with research in the field of disability studies that argues that placing the disability first (autistic person or blind person) reflects society's tendency to mark people with disabilities as entirely different (and therefore inferior) and place them in a separate group from "able" people.

> The philosophy of using person first language demonstrates respect for people with disabilities by referring to them first as individuals, and then referring to their disability when it is needed. This philosophy demonstrates respect by emphasizing what people can do by focusing on their ability rather than their disability and by distinguishing the person from the disability. (Blaska 1993)

Using person-first language seems a straightforward option, except for the fact that others in the community, including many people with ASD as well as parents/caregivers of those with ASD disagree (Brown 2011a, 2011b; Dunn and Andrews 2015; Sinclair 1999). They argue that autism is an intrinsic and important part of themselves, their child(ren), or other loved one that should be recognized. Some individuals with autism prefer the identity-first terms *autistic* or *autistic person*. As with the deaf community, they want to embrace or even celebrate their difference and do not see autism as a disability. Some of these same advocates contest the use of the word *disorder* in autism spectrum disorder for the same reason—they argue that they are different, not disabled. However, others in the autism community, especially the parents/caregivers of individuals who cannot speak for themselves and will always require care and support, insist that the word "disorder" is necessary to reflect the experiences of their children and the severity of the challenges they face. Some with autism worry that if the term "disorder" is not employed, access to needed support services would be discontinued (Kenny et al. 2016).

Where does that leave us? Although we understand the points made by scholars in the disability studies community, we also think it is important to respect the point of view of the students themselves who are living with autism. In a recent article published in *American Psychologist* (2015), Dana Dunn and Erin Andrews suggest that professionals adopt the use of both person-first and identity-first language. Identity-first language should be used whenever a preference is known (either in the case of an individual or agreement across a particular community). Person-first language should be used when a preference is unknown and in professional publications. Since this book is aimed at an academic audience, we will primarily use the person-first language embraced by scholars and professionals (*student with autism* or *student on the spectrum*), but we will not completely eschew identity-first language (*autistic students*) especially in cases where the person-first language results in awkward syntax. We will also frequently use the phrase *students with ASD*, because autism spectrum disorder is the official terminology used by the DSM-5; however, we will not otherwise use the terms "disorder" or "disability" to describe students on the spectrum, unless we are referring to a disability that a student might have separate from their autism diagnosis, as with learning disabilities.

Neurodiversity

In this book, as much as possible, we will emphasize the idea of neuro diversity instead of focusing on autism as a disorder. The image on the cover of this book is actually a neurodiversity symbol. Students with ASD are part of a larger group of neurodiverse students on campus. Proponents of the neurodiversity movement argue that brain differences (including not only ASD but also ADHD, dyslexia, and others) are simply normal genetic variants that come with both strengths and weaknesses.

NEURODIVERSITY TERMINOLOGY

Neurotypical = the majority of people with typical brain functioning.

Neurodivergent = those with difference in brain functioning. Neurodivergent does not equal autistic, because neurodivergent is a wider group. Since this book addresses those with ASD specifically and not the wider neurodivergent population, we will use this term infrequently.

This concept of neurodiversity is related to a shift in disability studies that has been moving away from the medical model of disability (focus on what people cannot do) to the social model (focus on how society's structure and biases limit what people can do) (Kapp et al. 2013; Lawrence 2013). When looking at ASD through the lens of neurodiversity, the focus shifts from seeing it as a problem that needs to be cured, to working to develop acceptance and accommodations to help everyone be successful. From the point of view of neurodiversity, autistic students are simply another group of diverse students with some specific needs that librarians and library staff are likely to encounter on campus, just as we might work with veterans, first-generation students, or nontraditional students.

Asperger's and High-Functioning Autism

Most librarians will be familiar with the term "Asperger's" or "Asperger's syndrome." We will not be using this term, simply because it was eliminated as a separate diagnosis in the DSM-5 in 2013. However, it will pop up occasionally because it was frequently used in research prior to that date. You may well encounter individuals who were diagnosed as having Asperger's prior to the DSM-5 and still self-identify that way. "High-functioning" autism is a term that has also frequently appeared in scholarship. It is employed because when looking at autism as a spectrum from a research perspective, there often needs to be a way of identifying where the participants of a study fall on that spectrum. College students with ASD would be considered "high functioning" because they have the abilities and skills needed to not only graduate from high school but also be accepted to college. Nevertheless, we will not be using this term, because we feel its use is rather demeaning to the wider group of those with ASD—any person who is not "high functioning" must then by default be "low functioning," which is a very pejorative way of thinking about someone. The most recent DSM (2013) roughly breaks down the spectrum into three "severity levels," based on the level of perceived deficits in the two main diagnostic criteria (social communication and restrictive, repetitive behavior) and reflecting the level of support needed by that individual. Level 3 "requiring very substantial support" is the most severe, and Level 1 "requiring support" is the least. Although we have not noticed these levels being employed in research, we think it is fair to assume that most college students with ASD would be diagnosed at Level 1.

So, What Should I Say?

Our best advice in all cases of working with students with autism is to listen to how a student refers to himself or herself and use that language. When in doubt, simply ask. One topic that will be addressed repeatedly throughout this book is that most people on the spectrum prefer and respond best to direct (even blunt) communication. You are more likely to offend by using the wrong language than by asking what someone prefers. If in doubt, use person-first language as your default—student with ASD/autism.

SCOPE AND OVERVIEW

This book is narrowly focused on working with college students with ASD in an academic setting. Although we do address student workers with ASD in Chapter 5 on employment, we are not addressing the broader topic of librarians and other library staff with ASD. For sources on that topic, please see the Recommended Reading section at the end of this introduction.

The book is divided into six chapters. Chapter 1 is dedicated to summarizing the most common characteristics of ASD (both strengths and weaknesses), as defined by the DSM-5, but with a focus on the characteristics that are most likely to affect a college student's success and their relationship with the library/library staff. Each subsequent chapter is dedicated to a different area of academic library services. In each, we review and summarize the existing research in a given area, pulling out what is most pertinent to librarians and library staff. Each chapter includes concrete strategies that can be employed in working with students with ASD. Whenever possible, we have incorporated local contributions—those of the students in our own university's autism support program in **Student Voices** segments and also that of our program's director, Cherie Fishbaugh, MA, BCBA, BS-L (PA). Cherie serves as our own personal expert, and her guidance and advice have been invaluable to us. She graciously agreed to contribute to this book by providing suggestions that appear in **Thoughts/ Tips from Our Expert** boxes in several chapters. Each chapter section ends with a selection of **Recommended Reading**—a short, annotated bibliography of books, chapters, or articles to read (or share with students, staff, or faculty). We have tried to select sources that not only provide additional information but are also written in general language and an appealing manner.

RECOMMENDED READING

Eng, Alice. 2017, June 28. "Neurodiversity in the Library: One Librarian's Experience." *In the Library with the Lead Pipe.* http://www.inthe librarywiththeleadpipe.org/2017/neurodiversity-in-the-library/

> This article is an interview with Charlie Remy, an academic librarian with ASD. He describes his own experiences and discusses issues related to neurodiversity in academic libraries.

Kenny, Lorcan, Caroline Hattersley, Bonnie Molins, Carole Buckley, Carol Povey, and Elizabeth Pellicano. 2016. "Which Terms Should Be Used to Describe Autism? Perspectives from the UK Autism Community." *Autism: The International Journal of Research and Practice* 20, no. 4: 442–462.

> If you want to know more about the debate around the language for describing autism, read this fantastic article. It provides an excellent discussion of the person-first versus identity/disability-first debate, before moving into the survey results. The many quotes from participants and the discussion do an excellent job of elucidating the many sides of a complex issue.

Lawrence, Emily. 2013. "Loud Hands in the Library: Neurodiversity in LIS Theory & Practice." *Progressive Librarian,* no. 41: 98–109.

> Written by a neurodivergent librarian, this article discusses neurodiversity from a library standpoint. It includes discussions of the various models of disability and the potential role of librarians in promoting a neurodiversity approach.

> There are also a number of autobiographies written by individuals with ASD, which would make good additions to an academic library's collection.

Temple Grandin

Thinking in Pictures: My Life with Autism
Temple Grandin: How the Girl Who Loved Cows Embraced Autism and Changed the World

Naoki Higashida

The Reason I Jump: The Inner Voice of a Thirteen-Year-Old Boy with Autism

Dawn Prince-Hughes

Songs of the Gorilla Nation: My Journey through Autism
Aquamarine Blue 5: Personal Stories of College Students with Autism

John Elder Robison
Be Different: My Adventures with Asperger's and My Advice for Fellow Aspergians, Misfits, Families, and Teachers
Look Me in the Eye: My Life with Asperger's

Liane Holliday Willey
Pretending to be Normal: Living with Asperger's Syndrome

ONE

Autism Spectrum Disorder: What Librarians and Staff Need to Know

Autism spectrum disorder (ASD) is defined by the *Diagnostic and Statistical Manual of Mental Disorders* (DSM-5) as "persistent impairment in reciprocal social communications and social interaction, and restricted, repetitive patterns of behavior, interests, or activities" (2013). This broad definition encompasses a range of criteria that can describe the behaviors and characteristics of an individual with ASD. However, not every person with ASD has all of these characteristics. Specifically, students with ASD in higher education may exhibit a range of these behaviors depending on the environment, circumstances, stress, and emotional state. In addition, life history plays a large role in how a student with ASD will respond to the experiences and demands in a higher education institution. Students with more academic and social supports in their earlier educational career may transition to college more easily than students without because they have learned skills that can be transferred to the college experience. It is important to stress that every student with autism is an individual with their own personality, traits, characteristics, and life experiences. One person with autism is not every person with autism, and all students with ASD should be treated as individuals.

The academic library is an inclusive campus location that provides a variety of resources, services, academic supports, and even a social gathering location for students. Library services and supports can often be found at a number of physical or virtual locations. Librarians and staff working in the academic library encounter both neurotypical and neurodivergent students at these service points. Students with ASD have unique characteristics that may present a challenge in communication when approaching and asking for assistance at library service points. When library staff are made aware of and are trained on the characteristics and behaviors of a student with ASD, it can help make communication and/or a service transaction more successful. Therefore, our first step is to provide an overview of the behaviors and characteristics of autism spectrum disorder. Typical characteristics that librarians and staff may encounter fall under three different categories: cognitive traits, social and communication skills, and motor skills. Although these categories were created by the author for the purpose of organizing this book, they tend to follow the categories in the DSM-5 and in scholarly literature. Regardless of severity or where an individual falls on the autism spectrum, all persons with ASD present with poor social interaction, language impairments, a limited interest in the environment, and sensory input sensitivities. We have found in both research and our own experience that there also exists groups of positive traits that are common among individuals with ASD. Therefore, after relevant sections, we have also included sections that highlight applicable strengths of individuals with ASD.

COGNITIVE TRAITS AND CHARACTERISTICS

Cognitive abilities play an important part in the intellectual and academic skill levels of students with ASD. Many individuals with ASD have normal or above-normal cognitive functioning (Sayman 2015). According to the CDC (2017), 44 percent of those diagnosed with ASD had average or above average intelligence. However, high levels of intelligence and cognitive functioning do not automatically mean success in college. Students with ASD struggle with executive functioning traits and skills that are essential to success in college. Executive functioning involves the prefrontal cortex and refers to processes that are associated with flexible, goal-directed behavior including planning, inhibition, working memory, and attention control (Banerjee 2006). Multitasking, time management, organizational skills, and study skills are some of the areas of difficulty for students with ASD (Anderson, Stephenson, and Carter 2017; Elias, Muskett, and White 2017; Geller and Greenburg 2009; Gobbo and Shmulsky 2014; Schindler et al. 2015;

QUICK LOOK: ASD COGNITIVE CHARACTERISTICS

- Difficulty multitasking
- Poor time management
- Poor organization and planning skills
- Difficulty with change and/or transitions

Shmulsky et al. 2017). Students with ASD often process information slowly and find it difficult to then organize that information into goals and outcomes. To further complicate things, ASD can also mean difficulties with distractibility, forgetfulness, and a decreased attention span (Schindler et al. 2015, p. 9). "Tasks or situations that are novel, unpredictable, or unfamiliar, such as those in a new college environment, have higher executive function demands than routine tasks" (Schindler et al. 2015). For example, engaging and learning in a 45-minute one-shot library instruction session can put to test the executive functioning skills of a student with ASD such as focus and attention span. Absorbing a large amount of new information in a short time frame can be difficult for students with ASD. Some other challenges present in students with ASD include inflexibility with thought patterns, especially abstract or ambiguous concepts (Anderson, Stephenson, and Carter 2017) and "difficulty with initiating and solving problems independently" (Elias, Muskett, and White 2017).

What Does This Mean for Libraries?

Library staff may encounter students having trouble paying attention during an instructional class, a tour, or a research help interaction. In addition, librarians may note that students may be late or forgetful of appointments, have difficulty organizing research sources, and have difficulty completing tasks. Service desks and other staff may interact with students who may be exhibiting signs of feeling overwhelmed due to not understanding how a process works or the rules of the particular service desk (e.g., checking a book out or making a photocopy or scan). However, once a student with ASD learns and understands the rules, they will adhere to them strictly. Finally, students with autism may lose focus or get easily distracted in situations that require sustained attention span like classroom instruction.

Positive Cognitive Traits

Although there are cognitive difficulties and challenges, there are also many areas of strength. Other than high levels of intelligence, students have a strong attention to detail (Anderson, Stephenson, and Carter 2017), excellent technological skills (Van Hees, Moyson, and Roeyers 2015), and demonstrate persistence (Drake 2014). In fact, Anderson, Carter, and Stephenson (2018) found that the most common strength was attention to detail. This trait is going to play a very important role in Chapter 5 on employment. Students with ASD often experience an intense interest in the subject they are studying and will develop an expertise in a particular subject area (Anderson, Stephenson, and Carter 2017). They exhibit a strong love for learning and enjoy sharing their expertise with others (Kirchner, Ruch, and Dziobek 2016), a trait that will return in Chapter 4 on instruction. One of the highest intellectual or cognitive traits found is creativity, showing originality and imagination when pursuing interests (Anderson, Carter, and Stephenson, 2018; Kirchner, Ruch, and Dziobek 2016). So while there may be difficulties with students with ASD initially transitioning to the college, many of them ultimately find the experience extremely rewarding.

STUDENT VOICES

I was excited and nervous at the same time! I was excited to not have to go to high school because that was torturous. I didn't have a lot of friends and classes were back to back. I didn't like the classes and what we had to learn, *Romeo and Juliet* amongst other Shakespearean works were not interesting to me. College was different because I get to choose my classes, the times, the professor. Choosing the professor is fantastic; they can make it or break it. Classes are much more interesting and many more options. I wish I knew [this] in high school[—it] isn't that bad. I am much more successful in college and MUCH more happier.—**Emma Billingsley**

SOCIAL SKILLS AND COMMUNICATION STYLES

As defined in the DSM-5 (2013), social and communication impairments associated with ASD are pervasive and sustained, meaning they remain with the individual throughout their life. There are a wide range of deficits ranging from complete lack of speech, language delays, to overly literal language. Often, when language abilities are present, the reciprocal use of language in social communication is impaired, meaning the back-and-forth conversational skills may not be present. Students who have been accepted to or are attending college tend to exhibit fewer communication deficits. They may have been diagnosed with less pervasive language deficits or may have had multiple supports and therapies to increase social communication abilities. Among the difficulties with social skills and communication, the most prevalent are poor eye contact; inability to initiate, conduct, or properly end a conversation; inconsistent and impulsive verbal and nonverbal behavior; and the inability to infer body language, humor, and sarcasm (Robledo, Donnellan, and Strandt-Conroy 2012; Sayman 2015; Schindler et al. 2015; Wolf, Brown, and Bork 2009). According to the DSM-5 (2013), individuals with ASD that have "superior language and intellectual abilities" as well as a specific interest or skill are more likely to be successful in college and beyond.

Many of the social cues and verbal and nonverbal behaviors in communication that come naturally to neurotypical individuals are not inherent in people with ASD. Students with ASD may have a difficult time understanding nonliteral language, sarcasm, when to initiate or end a conversation, as well as difficulty with reciprocating during a conversation. Additionally, a person with ASD may speak at high volume, sometimes being too loud for the social situation at hand (Zager and Alpern 2010). This can be problematic when in a library quiet zone or study area or even a computer lab where students are concentrating on writing papers or gathering research. Geller and Greenberg (2009) found that people with ASD can also be extremely talkative, with a conversation continuing for a long and possibly inappropriate amount of time. Social and communication impairments are a defining characteristic of ASD that we will be returning to throughout the book.

 **QUICK LOOK: ASD SOCIAL COMMUNICATION CHARACTERISTICS**

- Poor eye contact
- Lack of facial expressions, speech intonation, or gestures
- Difficult responding to social cues
- Speaking loudly
- No sharing of emotions
- Absent social interest

What Does This Mean for Libraries?

Since the library tends to be a very social place centered around service and communication, students with ASD may find it difficult to initially communicate with librarians and staff. Also, service and research help locations in the library may be difficult for students with autism to approach and converse with to meet a need. Some tips on this will be provided in Chapter 3 on research help. Chapter 4 on instruction will provide guidance for librarians doing any type of face-to-face instruction. Chapter 5 on employment will focus on how to communicate with student workers with ASD. Chapter 6 will discuss training of staff and outreach to students with ASD or campus autism support programs. In general, being aware of and trained on best communication practices with students with ASD is essential to successful student interactions.

Positive Social-Emotional Traits

Just as there are positive cognitive traits in those with ASD, there are also positive social-emotional character traits. In a 2016 study by Kirchner, Ruch, and Dziobek, results found that the top three interpersonal strengths in individuals with ASD are kindness, teamwork, and fairness, and the top three emotional strengths are zest, hope, and bravery (2016). The study found that individuals with ASD have fewer social stereotypes and do not feel pressure to abide by social rules or neurotypical standards of reputation. Persons with ASD are fair and lawful, often basing decisions and judgments on rules. These results are further supported by an earlier study that found the five highest strengths of individuals with ASD were open-mindedness, love of learning, fairness, curiosity, and authenticity (Samson and Antonelli 2013). So while it may be difficult to initially communicate with a person with ASD, some of the most admirable traits of individuals are found in this group, making it worth taking the extra time to communicate with and get to know these students.

MOTOR SKILLS AND REPETITIVE BEHAVIORS

Although the DSM-5 does not note specific deficits with motor skills, individuals with ASD find they experience difficulty with certain physical movements. One area of difficulty is in writing skills (Anderson,

Stephenson, and Carter 2017; Schindler et al. 2015). Handwriting tends to be poor in students with ASD, and "they may find it helpful to type up assignments and exams" (Robertson and Ne'eman 2008) rather than handwrite notes or assignments. This may most often be seen when communicating with students with ASD at a service desk in the library. Meeting with a librarian for research help can involve taking some notes or writing down specific instructions. Difficulties in taking notes can impact interactions at service desks (especially reference/research help) as well as classroom settings. Additionally, it is not seen as hand-holding to write down the instructions for the student so that they may refer to them at a later time when working on research individually.

Individuals with ASD also report difficulty controlling, executing and/or combining movements or keeping their body still (Elwin et al. 2013; Robledo, Donnellan, and Strandt-Conroy 2012). There can be a lack of coordination, and individuals with ASD often find it difficult to execute more than one physical action or movement at a time. These physical movements coupled with social and conversational interactions are behaviors that neurotypical people may notice but are not knowledgeable about. This can lead to library staff misinterpreting the body language or movements of a student with ASD. Training staff is discussed further in Chapter 6, but if a situation arises where an employee or student worker reports unusual or odd behavior, it may be an opportunity to educate and inform on the spot. Although staff are certainly not psychologists or trained to diagnose any one behavior, it is important to be knowledgeable about the different physical movements or behaviors that a student with ASD might have so as not to overreact or create an awkward or heightened situation.

Restricted, repetitive patterns of behavior are other key indicators of ASD. They can encompass physical, emotional, and behavioral characteristics. One of the primary characteristics is a need for everything to be the same and an inflexible adherence to routines or patterns of behavior (DSM-5 2013). Individuals with ASD do best with predictable routines. This trait will appear again in our instruction and employment chapters. Repetitive motor movements are characterized by movements without a purpose like hand flapping or waving, body rocking, or head banging. These behaviors can increase when a person with ASD experiences frustration or stress. Individuals diagnosed with ASD often have a preoccupation with nonfunctional objects and narrow or unusual patterns of interest (South, Ozonoff, and McMahon 2005). An individual with ASD may become focused on one object for a long period of time, such as the feel of fabric or

QUICK LOOK: ASD MOTOR SKILL CHARACTERISTICS

- Poor handwriting
- Lack or difficulty in physical coordination and body movements

other surfaces. Repetitive behavior symptoms can present difficulties for students with ASD, as they tend to be fixed and inflexible and individuals do not adapt to change easily. Hyper- and hyporeactivity to sensory input is another diagnostic symptom of autism spectrum disorder and will be discussed in more detail in Chapter 3.

What Does This Mean for Libraries?

Just as with social skills, it is essential that library staff are also trained and knowledgeable about the particular motor skill difficulties and repetitive movement behaviors that students with ASD may exhibit. For example, having understanding and patience to assist a student with ASD through a research help process where they may need to write down notes or ideas will help them be successful in the long term. It may take a student with ASD longer to record notes or the process of research that you are explaining. Additionally, giving directions in the library from a service desk may take longer and writing them down for the student would probably be best. Further, having understanding and patience when observing repetitive movement behaviors is extremely important. Giving students the appropriate space to feel comfortable in doing these behaviors makes them feel welcome and safe in the library.

NEEDS WHEN TRANSITIONING TO COLLEGE

Although neurotypical students transitioning to college can experience difficulties in adjusting to their new environment, students with ASD have an even harder time because of the difficulties with social communication skills and executive functioning. One of the first things new students do is seek out friendships or connections with other students. This can be a difficult and terrifying task for students with ASD because they lack an innate understanding of the social norms of approaching and conversing with others. Also, navigating not just one building but an entire campus of buildings, each with a different purpose, can lead to feelings of stress and anxiety. Experiences in classroom settings or campus opportunities that require organizing information and managing time can be difficult as well. One of the big responsibilities of college is learning how to manage and schedule time, set priorities, and meet deadlines. These are all executive functioning tasks, the lack of which is a significant trait of a student with autism, and which can result in stress and difficulties transitioning to college.

STUDENT VOICES

When transitioning to college it was hard. I went from high school of knowing everyone and where everything was located to starting from square one. I didn't know anyone. I had to make new friends; none of [my] friends came to West Chester. To help, I found that joining organizations and getting involved was extremely beneficial.—**Zach G.**

Higher education is a less structured environment than high school for students with ASD. Students with autism struggle to adjust to self-advocating, have difficulty socializing, and need more help with organization and time management, as well as developing routines (Elias and White 2018; Geller and Greenberg 2009; Gillespie-Lynch et al. 2017; Kuder and Accardo 2017). Time management is one of the major issues for students with ASD in college. Without support, students found they tended to procrastinate and at times, did not complete assignments, especially those with long-term deadlines (Knott and Taylor 2014). College students with ASD "may require assistance with planning, organizing, prioritizing, and scheduling their college course work" (Robertson and Ne'eman 2008) as well as help with "understanding directions and requesting help" (Geller and Greenberg 2009).

> The lack of structure and routines inherent in college life present difficulties for college students with ASD. Problems organizing information and planning can impact academic performance and contribute to the stress and anxiety that many students report. (Kuder and Accardo 2017)

In the end, understanding the challenges that college students have so that we can support them in successfully transitioning into college and through their college career should be the goal. One of the main themes of this book is that academic libraries and the people who work in them have an important role to play in the success of college students with autism.

Many students with ASD have had years of supports throughout their educational history. These supports often disappear at high school graduation. Once in college, a student needs to self-identify and often advocate for themselves in what is a new, exciting, and sometimes confusing environment. Just like any college student, students with ASD have a greater chance of success in college if supports are in place. Also, just like any college student, success for those with ASD is defined not just by getting good grades or passing classes but also by socializing, becoming more independent on campus, increasing involvement in campus activities, securing and keeping employment or internships, and of course, graduating. Success rates are higher when autism supports or programs are in place at an academic institution. Rates are even higher when campus departments engage in and collaborate with the programs (Schall, Wehman, and Carr 2014). According to a study by Hillier et al. (2017), "participants mentioned a range of benefits related to improved academic skills and greater knowledge of the university and resources available on campus."

What Does This Mean for Libraries?

We believe that the library is an essential campus resource that can contribute to the success of college students with autism. Each chapter in the remainder of this book focuses on a way students with ASD may interact with and utilize the library as well as ways the library can help (see Chapter 6 for information on academic supports and library outreach and programming).

A Library-Specific Example

Here is one example of how libraries may need to change their approach to support students with ASD. We want all students to use our libraries; however, students might not use the library as a resource because "decreased self-determination skills can affect a student's ability to navigate the college system and to interact successfully with faculty and with college staff" (Schindler et al. 2015). We challenge you to try thinking about your own library from the point of view of a new college student with ASD. Does your campus have more than one library? How do students know which library to use? Does your library have multiple types and locations of service points, each with a different set of rules or expectations? Although all students may wonder where they should go and who should they talk to, this can feel particularly overwhelming and confusing to students with ASD. Processing the steps or rules of engaging at service points can take time for them. Understanding directions and requesting help is an area of weakness for people with ASD (Geller and Greenberg 2009). In many college settings, this can present difficulties but especially in the library, as points of service require initiating contact and asking for assistance, whether it is a book on reserve or for research help. As we become more knowledgeable about students with ASD, libraries can make changes that allow us to serve as a campus location that can help make the transition to college smoother, less stressful, and more successful.

STUDENT SUCCESS

Students with autism spectrum disorder want and are extremely capable of attending and graduating from higher education institutions (Glennon 2016). In general, college students with ASD self-report high levels of academic success but also report difficulties with social experiences and executive functioning tasks such as time management and study skills (Sarrett 2017). The success rates of college students with autism as a specific disability category have not been reported and studied in great detail. This is most likely due to the very recent rise in the population attending higher education institutions in recent years and does not change the fact that, as for all college students, we want to see success—in classes, research, social interactions, graduation, and employment. Providing and being involved in support programming will greatly increase the success of students with ASD in college. "Security and continuity through transitions, education, and employment as means of broadening opportunities, and environments where young adults with autism were valued and supported" increases positive outcomes and success in higher education (Sosnowy, Silverman, and Shattuck 2017).

For anyone to be successful, but especially students with autism, support needs to include more than just academic skills (Knott and Taylor 2014). When working with a diverse student body, it is beneficial to be aware and trained on best practices for communicating with and assisting students.

In a 2012 study by Robledo et al., a study participant noted that they wanted understanding and support, especially without criticism. Many students with ASD feel isolated and/or misunderstood (Kuder and Accardo 2017; Robledo, Donnellan, and Strandt-Conroy 2012) because the focus on interactions is often based on the outward behavior (Robledo, Donnellan, and Strandt-Conroy 2012). Results of a 2014 study (Schriber, Robins, and Solomon 2014) found that individuals with ASD are aware of their own personalities and the social, emotional, and physical difficulties that arise from these traits. This correlates with high levels of depression and anxiety in individuals with ASD. With the self-awareness comes a sense of social isolation and anxiety that can result in depression (Anderson, Stephenson, and Carter 2017; Jackson et al. 2018; Knott and Taylor 2014; Kuder and Accardo 2017). By increasing awareness, understanding, and training on college campuses as well as developing academic, social, and emotional support programs to college students with ASD, the potential for academic success increases.

CONCLUSION: WHAT DOES THIS MEAN FOR LIBRARIES?

The library can play a vital role in the success of students with ASD in higher education. Through research help, library instruction, space planning, employment opportunities, and outreach efforts librarians can assist students with ASD. Not only can we support their academic success, but we can assist in teaching independence, communication skills, time management, and organization skills. This is a valuable opportunity for the library to be a part of the overall success of students with ASD in higher education. We hope that this book will provide academic librarians and staff the knowledge, resources, and tools to be an integral part of the growth and success of college students with autism spectrum disorder.

RECOMMENDED READING

Geller, Lynda L., and Michael Greenberg. 2009. "Managing the Transition Process from High School to College and Beyond: Challenges for Individuals, Families, and Society." *Social Work in Mental Health* 8, no. 1: 92–116. https://doi.org/10.1080/15332980902932466.

Though this article is nearly 10 years old, Geller and Greenberg have written an excellent and comprehensive piece covering every aspect of the transition from high school to college for a student with autism spectrum disorder.

Hoffman, Jan. 2016, November 19. "Along the Autism Spectrum, a Path through Campus Life." *The New York Times.*

> Although we did not cite this article within this book, it provides an excellent and interesting picture of the life and characteristics of a student with ASD.

Kirchner, Jennifer, Willibald Ruch, and Isabel Dziobek. 2016. "Brief Report: Character Strengths in Adults with Autism Spectrum Disorder without Intellectual Impairment." *Journal of Autism and Developmental Disorders* 46, no. 10: 3330–3337. https://doi.org/10.1007/s10803-016 -2865-7.

> We particularly like this article because it discussed the character strengths of individuals with autism spectrum disorder. We feel that having the knowledge and understanding of strengths is an important piece of working with students with ASD.

Sayman, Donna M. 2015. "I Still Need My Security Teddy Bear: Experiences of an Individual with Autism Spectrum Disorder in Higher Education." *Learning Assistance Review* 20, no. 1: 77–98. https:// eric.ed.gov/?id=EJ1058012.

> This is a qualitative study of one woman with ASD and her experience transitioning from high school and navigating college and employment.

Volkmar, Fred R., Brian Reichow, and James C. McPartland. 2014. *Adolescents and Adults with Autism Spectrum Disorders.* New York: Springer.

> Although this book also contains a good overview of the characteristics of ASD, Chapter 3 in particular provides a helpful summary on the transition process and outcomes for students with ASD.

TWO

Sensory Issues, Physical Environment, and Library Spaces

In 2013, the fifth edition of the *Diagnostic and Statistical Manual of Mental Disorders* (DSM-5) included, for the first time, sensory processing abnormalities as one of the characteristics of autism. Repetitive and fixed interest behaviors were expanded to include hyper- and hyporeactivity to sensory input or unusual interests in sensory aspects of the environment (DSM-5 2013). Hyporesponsiveness is an underreaction to environmental stimuli (heat, smells, flavors, pain, or hunger) and hyperresponsiveness (noises and visual aspects that most people do not notice) is an overreaction to environmental stimuli (DSM-5 2013; Elwin et al. 2012). Additionally, individuals with ASD may crave or seek out specific sensory experiences. Examples given in the DSM-5 include indifference to pain/temperature, adverse response to certain sounds or textures, excessive smelling or touching of objects, and a visual fascination with lights or movement. Prior to 2013, autism spectrum disorder was defined and diagnosed based on social deficits and restricted or repetitive behavioral characteristics alone. Researchers were unsure if the sensory abnormalities were a cause or effect of the other symptoms and/or characteristics of ASD. In a study by Horder et al. (2014) they found that "abnormalities with sensory processing and anxiety symptoms are correlated, yet distinct, phenomena . . . confirming the link between sensory experiences and autism across the spectrum." Another study (Otto-Meyer et al. 2018) found that the symptoms of ASD come from the difficulty in distinguishing signals from noise in the brain. Finally,

Robertson and Simmons (2012) found that extreme responses to sensory experiences are more common in individuals with increased traits or symptoms of autism spectrum disorder. Sensory symptoms are often subjective and sometimes not easily observed, as they may be dependent on factors such as stress and anxiety, or attributes of the physical space the individual is in. However, the sensitivities impact the daily routines and experiences of a person with autism spectrum disorder.

Those sensory processing issues can make interacting with the physical space of a library a much different experience for students with ASD than for neurotypical students. The academic library can pose both challenges and opportunities for students with ASD. From finding quiet study spaces, social gathering spaces, or fulfilling class requirements to gathering research or other class materials, there are multiple needs and uses. In addition to the obvious services, academic libraries are currently being utilized or designed to serve as many needs as possible, including writing centers, makerspaces, and tutoring. Within those spaces, library administration and staff are finding they need to be flexible—movable furniture, increased access to electrical outlets, and multiple services at one desk (Staines 2012). A student with ASD can find it overwhelming to navigate the physical space of a library to accomplish these goals. Further complicating this is the wide variety of library architecture designs. From modern to historic, libraries often have dark, quiet spaces as well as large, open, and boisterous spaces. In some cases, small changes in the library can provide a supportive environment for students with ASD to study, communicate with staff, and socialize with peers. Recognizing the different physical space needs of students with ASD will help increase success and provide them with another inviting and inclusive environment on campus.

HOW STUDENTS WITH ASD USE THE LIBRARY

Although research is growing in the areas of how college students with ASD are utilizing campus supports, activities, and offices, there is little research on how they are specifically using the library. We know that students in general utilize the library for a variety of reasons—studying, gathering research, group work, library instruction classes, to visit a campus support like the writing center or tutoring services—and we can predict that students with ASD are doing the same. One thing that the research on how students with ASD use campus supports does show is that there is a need for more support programs for both academic and social-emotional needs to support student success (Jackson, Scott et al. 2018; Knott and Taylor 2014)—a topic we will return to in Chapter 6. We argue that the library should absolutely be an essential part of supports on campus. Academic libraries are in a unique position to offer both academic and social support to students with ASD.

One of the reasons college students with ASD are likely visiting the library is to engage in social interaction with peers. It provides a safe space to interact and have discussions with neurotypical students about class topics or projects. It also provides a positive experience to improve study habits and skills by observing and working with peers and library staff. On the other hand, some students with ASD visit the library to find a dark, quiet space free from noise and distractions. Unfortunately for those students, in a 2010 study Madriaga reported students with ASD found the university library an inaccessible place to study depending on the time of day. Most of the respondents in Madriaga's study reported that the library was too noisy and busy. Further, it has been found that high levels of noise can be more disruptive and have negative effects when a student with ASD is trying to focus on a task (Landon, Shepherd, and Lodhia 2016). This aligns with the broader research on sensory sensitivities in individuals with ASD. It is difficult for persons with ASD to filter out stimuli and concentrate or focus on a task at hand (Elwin et al. 2013; Smith and Sharp 2013). Libraries can unknowingly contribute to this difficulty with the amount of visual and auditory stimuli that occurs in the building. Many students with ASD have had therapies and supports prior to transitioning to college that have provided them with strategies to manage difficult or overwhelming sensory experiences. You may see students who will calm themselves down through physical activity (like walking around the library), using headphones to block out noise, or simply avoiding places or situations that are too overwhelming (Elwin et al. 2013; Kanakri et al. 2017; Smith and Sharp 2013). Ultimately, the goal for academic libraries should be to communicate with students on the autism spectrum early about different areas in the library that may be more conducive rather than having them avoid the library. We want all students to feel comfortable and successful when using all of the services and resources the library has to offer.

Academic libraries are no longer a stereotypical place of quiet and solitude. They have become a central campus location for socialization, group work, study space, collaborative and instructional meetings, makerspaces, and more. On many campuses, the library is a hub of activity on par with the student union or student activity center. In general, academic libraries tend to be noisier than in the past. Changes have been consciously made in order to make academic libraries more appealing. We are proud of our busy, vibrant libraries! Yet these very changes can have a negative impact on this particular group of students. Unfortunately, research on how students with ASD use the library is severely lacking. Both Kanakri et al. (2017) and Landon et al. (2016) found that the impact of noise and stimuli on persons with ASD is also sparse. However, from the broader literature, we know that busy, loud spaces can make it more difficult for students with ASD to find the type of space or location they need for studying or concentrated task work. We need to consider their needs and look for simple things that can be done to support them.

STUDENTS WITH ASD AND THE PHYSICAL LIBRARY

New situations, activities, and information are overwhelming to students with ASD (Anderson, Carter, and Stephenson 2018; Madriaga 2010; Van Hees et al. 2015). Libraries are notorious for providing *all* the information—there is a lot to look at, a lot to read, and a lot to process. This can cause feelings of stress and anxiety in all students. Over half the respondents in a recent study (Anderson, Carter, and Stephenson 2018) reported that their sensitivities to "noise, light or smells on campus sometimes interfered with their ability to study or cope on campus." Take, for instance, the impact of noise. Students with ASD get easily distracted by high levels of activity and noise (Anderson, Carter, and Stephenson 2018; Elwin et al. 2012; Kanakri et al. 2017; Landon et al. 2016; Madriaga 2010; Schindler and Cajiga 2015). Sounds that neurotypical students do not hear or can tune out are the same background noises that may cause students with ASD to have trouble concentrating and communicating. This can lead to feelings of stress, confusion, fatigue, or annoyance (Landon et al. 2016). Some typical sounds or noises that can feel overwhelming or disruptive to a student with ASD include the buzz or flickering of fluorescent lights, humming of computers or other electronic devices, typing on a keyboard, ticking of clocks, doors opening and shutting, and even student conversations. Students with ASD can easily suffer from sensory overload in situations with a lot of sounds (Van Hees,

Moyson, and Roeyers 2015). When there is a lot of visual and auditory stimulation, students with ASD find it extremely difficult to concentrate, which, in turn, has an impact on academic success (Kanakri et al. 2017).

Think about your own library from the point of view of someone with sensitivity to noise. Libraries are inundated with background noises—multiple student conversations, plethora of electronic equipment like copiers, scanners, and computers, as well as unpredictable noises at library service locations. All of these noises can create a stressful environment or experience for students with ASD. Most background or extraneous noises are unwanted or bothersome to students with ASD, and they will avoid areas with these sounds (Cherney 2017; Kanakri et al. 2017). Although we have focused on noise as our specific example, the same holds true for other types of sensitivities such as visual, tactile, or smells. Individuals with ASD often find artificial lighting such as fluorescent and strobe lights bothersome and, at times, even painful to look at (Robledo, Donnellan, and Strandt-Conroy 2012). The feel of certain fabrics or textures and strong smells or odors may also evoke a similar response (Robledo, Donnellan, and Strandt-Conroy 2012). Library staff might observe that students engage in self-stimulatory or self-treatment behaviors and strategies when experiencing a stress response to noises or sounds in the library. Students may be seen pacing in one location, flapping their arms or hands, coughing repetitively, humming, covering their ears, hyperventilating, or just general restlessness (Kanakri et al. 2017; Stiegler and Davis 2010). It is important to be aware of these behaviors and understand that they are simply a response to overwhelming stimuli.

If a student with ASD anticipates or encounters a location or situation that is uncomfortable sensory wise, they may either leave the situation suddenly or routinely avoid that location (Landon, Shepherd, and Lodhia 2016). Van Hees et al. (2015) found that participants in their study avoided the library specifically due to sensory overload. This had an impact on their social lives and academic achievement as they were experiencing fewer social interactions and avoiding a campus location of academic support. Students with ASD may choose to not study or use resources at the library, and this is exactly what we want to prevent. Although the library may be a location with stressful noise and stimuli, there are things that can be done to support students with ASD so that they view the library as a welcoming, useful, and most importantly, stress-free space. Finding ways to create a safe and positive learning or gathering space for students with

ASD will assist in their social growth as well as help them be successful in their college career.

UNIVERSAL DESIGN IN HIGHER EDUCATION: PHYSICAL SPACES

Universal Design was invented by Ronald L. Mace of North Carolina State University in the 1970s. It began as a movement in architecture and design and thus was originally developed to address the physical world. The basic tenet of Universal Design calls for "the design of products and environments to be usable by all people, to the greatest extent possible, without the need for adaptation or specialized design" (Center for Universal Design 2008). In other words, if a designer thinks about people with different abilities when they initially design an object, more people will be able to use it. The classic design example is the curb cut. Although a person may think of it as being designed to assist a person in a wheelchair, it is also quite useful for parents pushing strollers or someone using a dolly or pulling a wagon.

Universal Design has become an important and timely topic in higher education. Essentially, higher education institutions are becoming more aware and more receptive to creating learning communities and spaces that are inclusive and equitable to all learners regardless of age, gender, race, socioeconomic status, and disabilities. According to the National Center for Education Statistics (United States Department of Education 2016), approximately 11 percent of the student body in colleges and universities have a disability. Many disabilities are considered "invisible," including autism spectrum disorder, meaning there is not an obvious physical disability. Although Chapter 4 will introduce Universal Design for Instruction, this section will explore Universal Design for physical spaces, specifically in regard to students with autism spectrum disorder.

Universal Design for physical spaces involves evaluating an existing situation, making an assessment on accommodations, and removing barriers (Burgstahler 2015). Some obvious accommodations for those with a disability would be automatic doors, ramps, lower desks, and braille signage. For students with autism spectrum disorder, Universal Design accommodations in physical spaces may be more subtle and therefore not readily apparent. This does not matter, however, because Universal Design eliminates the differentiation of disabilities and creates physical spaces and designs that are accessible to all. One recent article (Cherney 2017) applies the tenets of Universal Design to an academic writing center. Many of the

QUICK LOOK: UNIVERSAL DESIGN IN HIGHER EDUCATION FOR PHYSICAL SPACES

- Consider diversity issues during evaluation and planning.
- Appearance—create an appealing environment to all.
- Physical access—create welcoming and barrier-free entries.
- Furniture and fixtures—able to be used by all.
- Information resources and technology—accessible to all.
- Safety—design to minimize risk to injury.
- Accommodations—develop procedures for taking requests. (Burgstahler 2015)

same characteristics addressed in the article apply to libraries as well. For example, fluorescent lighting, open spaces, and multiple conversations occurring at the same time are all marked as potentially problematic. Library administrators or staff can apply Universal Design by trying to adapt a space or the building to create multiple spaces in which all students, including those with ASD, can feel comfortable learning, studying, or conversing.

PROVIDING SPACES TO MEET THE NEEDS OF STUDENTS WITH ASD

Many studies and anecdotes provide information on the coping skills and strategies students with ASD use, rather than the implementation of physical or environmental solutions that can benefit all students (Kanakri et al. 2017). Academic library buildings may be very old and in need of a serious renovation or extremely new but geared toward a more active and boisterous space. Older academic libraries, especially those with architecture from the 1960s and 1970s, tend to have unusual floor plans, less adaptable spaces, and less natural light. Newer academic libraries tend to have large, open, and bright spaces that can be noisy. It is important that, no matter the age of the building, library administrators and staff look into ways they can improve their spaces to provide the best experience for all students. We can and should get creative—working within the confines of the existing library space and structure. The academic library is an excellent campus location to provide a variety of learning and social spaces for students with ASD including calm, quiet, and, if able, nonfluorescent spaces. It is important to create and identify these quiet study spaces in the library. Library locations that support neurodiverse learners can contribute to the success and retention of students with ASD in college. Inclusive environments where ASD students feel supported increase independence and success (Hendrickson et al. 2017). Remember that the changes you make with students with ASD in mind may also very well be appreciated by other students as well—that is the whole idea behind Universal Design!

STUDENT VOICES

It was also beneficial to have set up times to visit the library and other resources across campus to know where they were and how to access. I find the library to be a really great place to study and get work done; I'm productive there. It is quiet.—**Zach G.**

STRATEGIES AND IDEAS

Interior design goes beyond lighting and wall color. There are many elements of the "non-structural environment—such as furniture, colors, decorations, natural light, signage, electrical, mechanical" systems that help create the most functional and ASD supportive environment (Smith 2017). Regardless of the available library spaces and physical layout, color selection, correct lighting, security, interior comfort (temperature, humidity, noise control), durability of materials (furniture, flooring, shelving), and usability of technology all impact a student's experience in the library. In all of these, the most important thing is an understanding of how the space will be used and also in creating welcoming, comfortable spaces for all library users. For libraries that are constrained by their current building design and age, creating comfortable, universally friendly spaces that are conducive to the activity occurring in the space is still a viable solution. Rearranging furniture, painting walls, and adding signage are simple, less expensive ways to make positive changes in your building. If your library is lucky enough to be going through or in line for a major renovation or new building, we highly recommend consulting the information in the Staines book, included in the Recommended Reading at the end of the chapter. Below are some strategies you can try to implement.

Look for Ways to Reduce or Muffle Sound

Overall, studies are finding that there is a need for solutions to reduce auditory discomfort in busy and loud buildings or spaces (Kanakri et al. 2017; Robertson and Ne'eman 2008). In a study by Kanarki et al. (2017), the researchers found specific examples of the physical environment that would reduce noise levels, including carpeting, wood furniture, thick or acoustical walls, and transitional spaces. In the same study negative aspects were also observed. These included echoes, hard floors, metal furniture, light-colored walls, high ceilings, and no carpet. Carpets can be added to tile or wood floors to reduce echoes and loud noises, but the color of the carpeting should be chosen carefully (Staines 2012). Busy, overpowering colors and patterns are distracting and can feel overwhelming to students with ASD. Physical changes are not the only possibility. Our local expert, Cherie Fishbaugh, recommends having noise-canceling headphones available for borrowing and if possible, designated quiet areas. Our library has designated quiet floors, and we recommend these spaces to the students in our campus autism program. Cherie also notes that although elimination of all noise is not feasible, there are some noises to be mindful of when designating quiet spaces: lights, water fountains, elevators, printers, computer keyboards, phones, clocks, vents, and squeaky tables and chairs.

Update or Change Lighting

The use of soft or natural lighting is the best option (Elwin et al. 2012) as, according to our local expert, it is preferred by students with ASD because fluorescent lighting can cause feelings of pain or uncomfortableness in the eyes. It is also important to pay attention to glare and brightness (Staines 2012). This can be one of the more difficult things to change since most libraries have fixtures in place that are not easy or may be expensive to replace. Additionally, like most academic buildings libraries are frequently equipped with fluorescent lighting. Creating study or seating spaces near windows is an easy possibility and change to make.

Update or Change Colors

The aesthetic aspects of your library are important to pay attention to and are sometimes the easiest changes to make. Paint is one of the most inexpensive ways to update and change a room while also having an impact on how people feel when they are using or visiting a space. Investigate or research colors that have a positive effect on the learning experiences of college students. Colors should be complementary and provide direction and continuity throughout the building, helping users identify spaces (Kinnaer, Baumers, and Heylighen 2016; Staines 2012).

Remove Distracting Clutter

Other studies encourage the removal of extraneous decorations and detail because they "provide irrelevant stimuli" that can be extremely distracting for students with autism (Bogdashina 2004; Cai and Richdale 2016; Kinnaer, Baumers, and Heylighen 2016). For example, our own library recently implemented a project to reduce wall hangings or pictures, impractical furniture, and signs that were irrelevant or contained excessive verbiage. The library staff was so used to the objects that we did not notice when they were removed! Yet, this is exactly the sort of clutter that might be very distracting to a student with ASD. The next step in the project is to put up fewer, but more effective signs in relevant places in the building. Our library is lucky to house an instructional media and technology center where we can print our own signs for minimal cost.

Signage and Building Navigation

As we introduced in Chapter 1, individuals with autism spectrum disorder work best in predictable and structured environments and usually work on a set schedule (Bogdashina 2004). One of the problems with the transition to college is that students with ASD are put in an environment where everything is new at the same time—people, situations, and spaces—which results in very high executive functioning demands (Schindler et al. 2015). The library is just one of the many new places they need to learn to navigate. Students with ASD are visual learners and navigate places and spaces best with visual cues or images. These are extremely helpful to students with ASD because they provide comfort and less stress to be able to easily identify and navigate a physical space. Signage is important, but images or colors that go with the directional or locational signs are ideal. One architectural element that is starting to be used in many academic libraries and subscribes to Universal Design principles is color coding specific areas of the library. This helps all students orient themselves within the library and identifies spaces by visual signs and colors. Additionally, landmarks can provide a predictable pattern for students with ASD to navigate their way around a campus or building. To facilitate this, identify and map these locations in a handout and/or on a web guide to make the knowledge available to all (Kinnaer, Baumers, and Heylighen 2016). Incorporating these types of strategies discussed above gives a sense of familiarity and order, which reduces stress, increases comfort, and thereby increases student success. Once again, this is a fine example of Universal Design. Although we are suggesting signage and maps as a specific strategy for supporting students with ASD, this is actually something that will positively impact the vast majority of your patrons.

Add a "Calm Space"

In Jennifer Sarrett's 2017 article, study participants "identified the library as a safe space on campus." This is fantastic news, but we can go even further and make a space in the library that is especially appealing to students with ASD. Although it is most likely not possible to restructure or modify all existing library spaces, how about creatively using even one small space as a designated "calm space" that would be beneficial for students with ASD? These spaces or locations can be used on a first come, first serve basis, or if more desirable, can be scheduled or reserved on request. Calm spaces are rooms with low lighting, low noise, and perhaps a policy of no perfume or strong smells that students with autism can access (Sarrett 2017). A mother summed up her son's college experience well, reporting his sensitivity to noise and clutter—"he is very sensitive to noise . . . quiet rooms are very, very much preferable, but not always possible. Walls without . . . too many distractions is [also] preferable" because it can lead to distraction, which in turn can lead to anxiety (Cai and Richdale 2016). Calm spaces should also have a variety of seating options, such as armchairs, ball chairs, beanbags, and comfortable floor seating. Additionally, there can be an area, or areas, of the room dedicated to people wanting to be in the space but not interact with others (Sarrett 2017). Another option would be to add a sensory room that provides different textures, lights, colors, and sounds, which provide a space to escape to (Kinnaer, Baumers, Heylighen 2016; Leekam et al. 2007; Smith and Sharp 2013).

TIPS FROM OUR EXPERT: SENSITIVITIES TO SENSORY STIMULI

Cherie Fishbaugh, MA, BCBA, BS-L (PA)

Students with autism often have extreme sensitivities to sensory stimuli. Providing a welcoming environment encompasses all the senses:

Sight: Natural light is best. Fluorescent lights may not only cause pain to the eyes, but also the humming sound can lead to great distraction and frustration. Have areas with little décor on the walls to distract student. Have areas clearly labeled.

Sound: Have designated quiet areas and access to noise-canceling headphones. Although elimination of all noise is not feasible, some items to be mindful of include lights, water fountains, elevators, printers, computer keyboards, phones, clocks, vents, and squeaky tables and chairs.

Touch: Be aware of fabric versus vinyl on chairs. The majority of our students requested fabric chairs instead of vinyl—not only due to sticking to vinyl but also the sound it makes. In addition, many students like to lounge in areas. Big chairs and movable ottomans with side tables are inviting.

CONCLUSION

Keep in mind that not all students with ASD have exactly the same needs. Although students with autism tend to prefer small spaces to reduce sensory stimuli, some do prefer open spaces so that they have a visual of the entire space. This allows for predictability but also the ability to distance themselves from others while at the same time, not isolating themselves from the possibility of social interactions (Kinnaer, Baumers, and Heylighen 2016). On the other hand, Schindler et al.'s 2015 study identified participants that felt overstimulated in big classrooms or lecture halls due to the large and less structured space. This resulted in distraction and a sense of discomfort for the students. The same can be said of the college library. Some modern libraries may have large, predictable, and structured spaces, but older libraries often have a variety of large and small spaces and less flow and structure of services. Creating neutral, predictable environments or spaces helps students with ASD adjust to and succeed in an academic library and hopefully, at college overall (Kinnaer, Baumers, and Heylighen 2016). Ultimately, the goal is to provide spaces and environments that give a sense of clarity and order and reduce stress to increase student success. Providing a variety of available study spaces in the library is important. Making the information on the location of these spaces well known is essential.

Also remember that in addition to taking steps to make your library inviting for students with ASD, you also need to make sure they learn about these spaces! Communicate quiet study spaces with the Office of Disability Services at your institution or, if one exists, with the campus autism program. Introduce this space to groups of students by offering a tour or hosting a small open house of the space. We will discuss this and other outreach strategies in more detail in Chapter 6. Another important thing to note is that it is necessary to give time for students to acclimate to the new environments or space (Cherney 2017). Once students are acclimated, stress levels decrease, which thereby decreases sensory symptoms or traits. This is exactly what we hope for as it opens the door for students with ASD to use both the library space and our many fantastic services. We want students with ASD to feel comfortable using our libraries, and we want them to return often to do so!

RECOMMENDED READING

Elwin, Marie, Lena Ek, Lars Kjellin, and Agneta Schröder. 2013. "Too Much or Too Little: Hyper- and Hypo-Reactivity in High-Functioning Autism Spectrum Conditions." *Journal of Intellectual and Developmental Disability* 38, no. 3: 232–241. https://doi.org/10.3109/13668250.2013.815694.

This article provides a good understanding of sensory conditions with autism disorder, how an individual with autism responds to sensory stimuli, and their coping strategies.

Kinnaer, Marijke, Stijn Baumers, and Ann Heylighen. 2016. "Autism-Friendly Architecture from the Outside in and the Inside out: An Explorative Study Based on Autobiographies of Autistic People." *Journal of Housing and the Built Environment* 31, no. 2: 179–195. https://doi.org/10.1007/s10901-015-9451-8.

Anecdotal and autobiographical material provide the basis for this excellent article on how students with autism feel in a variety of spaces and how they respond to the physical spaces. This article provides great material for understanding their experiences and needs.

Robledo, Jodi, Anne M. Donnellan, and Karen Strandt-Conroy. 2012. "An Exploration of Sensory and Movement Differences from the Perspective of Individuals with Autism." *Frontiers in Integrative Neuroscience* 6: article 107. https://doi.org/10.3389/fnint.2012.00107.

This is another excellent article that provides anecdotal evidence from individuals with autism. Through the study, the authors provide a good picture of the sensory experiences and responses of a person with autism as well as difficulties with communication.

Staines, Gail M. 2012. *Universal Design: A Practical Guide to Creating and Recreating Interiors of Academic Libraries for Teaching, Learning, and Research.* Oxford, UK: Chandos.

This book is a comprehensive resource for all aspects of Universal Design for physical spaces as well as strategies and ideas for changes including codes and standards.

THREE

Research Help (and Beyond)

Providing research assistance is a core function of many librarians in academic libraries. Whether it is at a reference/research help desk or via appointments for individual consultations, aiding students, faculty, and other patrons with research is a frequent (and often extremely rewarding) task. Therefore, this book would not be complete without a chapter dedicated to the potential struggles students with ASD may face when searching and selecting sources for research projects. This chapter will address those issues and provide strategies librarians can use to help them.

As the title indicates, providing research assistance to students with ASD is the focus of this chapter, but the reference desk is not the only place in the library that students with ASD will be found. Just like neurotypical students, they will also use other library service points and spaces for research, studying, and socializing. So, this chapter will also provide some information and strategies that apply to situations other than research help and to library employees other than librarians. If that is the information you need, then we suggest you go straight to the section titled Social Aspects of Research Assistance. It provides a lot of information that is applicable to interacting with individuals with ASD in general and ends with a section that focuses on other situations that may arise in the library. The second half of the chapter focuses on how executive functioning and other factors specific to autism can impact the research process for students with ASD and provides strategies that are very specific to providing research help.

Before we start examining the research process with regard to students with ASD, we need to directly address the scholarship, or in this case, the lack of scholarship in this area. There is a fair amount of research available on the topic of understanding how ASD affects the *writing* process—some of which is also applicable to the research process. However, most of that scholarship has been focused on students in the K–12 setting. Much less attention has been given to writing at the college level. Of that research, only a very small portion directly addresses academic, research-based writing. Even less scholarship has been published about librarians working with students with ASD in an academic environment. As a result, this particular chapter is less grounded in empirical research than others in this book. Many of the tips and insights we provide in this chapter are proven approaches, but they have been developed for use in other contexts. An example of this would be modeling, which is a widely used approach for helping individuals with ASD learn social skills, but which we are applying to the research process. Some of the ideas have been suggested to us by our campus expert and autism support program director, Cherie Fishbaugh. She has used her experience working with high school and college students on the spectrum to suggest strategies that might help librarians serve this particular group of students. Some of the approaches discussed are things we have incorporated into our own practices and found successful. Others are things we are still in the process of implementing.

SOCIAL ASPECTS OF RESEARCH ASSISTANCE

Research assistance is a social interaction. Anyone who has spent time at a help desk or done frequent in-office appointments knows how widely these interactions can vary based on many factors. Does the student know what they need? Can they express it? Have they had any sort of library instruction? How confident/able are they at using the research tools? Do they say a lot or almost nothing at all? How open are they to learning new skills? As part of the research interview librarians assess how much help a student needs, how much information and level of detail to give, when to provide extra help, and when to push a student to try strategies independently. Often, we make those decisions based only on a short conversation as part of the reference interview. Since difficulties with social interactions are a hallmark of ASD (see Chapter 1 for more details), a librarian working with a student with ASD will likely find that it impacts the research interview process.

But here is the conundrum. You probably will not know if a particular student who approaches the desk or sets up an appointment with you has

ASD. This is not a situation where the student is likely to self-disclose; nor should they be expected to do so. You may, however, suspect in many cases, based on cues you receive from the social interaction. Common clues would be the student's pattern of speech or inflection, lack of eye contact or facial expression, and unusual body language (DSM-5 2013). Since very few librarians are trained psychologists, we cannot diagnose a student with ASD, and it is rude to ask. So what can a librarian do when faced with a situation where they are making a guess as to what the student needs? The good news is that many of the strategies that we discuss in the chapter, while aimed at someone with ASD, are actually much more broadly applicable and would also support a wide range of students, including those with learning disabilities or differences and those who are just not particularly skilled communicators. We will be talking in detail in Chapter 4 about the concept of Universal Design for Instruction—incorporating teaching techniques from the start that benefit the broadest number of students. Although we are not trying to actually develop a Universal Design for Reference Services, the concept does transfer fairly well, as many research help interactions could be considered one-on-one mini instruction sessions.

One of the things you may notice when working with students with ASD is the unusual flow of conversation and lack of back-and-forth dialogue. Some students might provide you with very few cues and feedback (DSM-5 2013). You may need to initiate or guide the conversation and social interaction. For instance, we tend to look for eye contact in others as an indication that they are engaged in a conversation. We also look for physical or verbal feedback that indicates understanding. Nodding, asking questions, and murmured "uh huhs" or "okays" or "ahs" would all be examples. Not receiving that kind of feedback can be confusing and even a bit off-putting to someone who is neurotypical, because it may seem as if the student is not paying attention. However, a student with ASD may be quite engaged but just not producing those types of responses that are natural for most neurotypical adults. In these circumstances, you simply should ask more questions to get the feedback you need. *Does what I just showed you make sense? Do you want to see that again? What do you think of this source—is it something you could use? Are you comfortable trying this on your own? Is that enough for now, or do you want to keep working on this?* This is an approach that we have had success with, because it is helpful with any student who is not providing a lot of feedback for a variety reasons—maybe they are not particularly interested in learning how to research, are overwhelmed by the process, or are just plain shy and uncomfortable talking to a librarian.

The other extreme you may occasionally run into is a student who draws out the research interaction too long. Perhaps the student has a lot of questions. Or perhaps the conversation led into the topic that the student is particularly interested in. As discussed in Chapter 1, cognitive strengths of those with ASD include a love of learning and a passionate interest in certain subjects. Given that individuals with ASD can have difficulty forming social relationships, especially when transitioning to a new environment like college, they may simply be happy to have found someone who is willing to talk to them about an interest. Although most librarians are quite friendly and enjoy talking to students, we all reach a point when we need to end a consultation. Perhaps there is another student waiting to be helped, a chat you put on hold, you simply have work to do, or it is the end of the day and you need to go home! With neurotypical students, you could signal the end of a session by using subtle cues, either verbal (e.g., "let's wrap this up," "I think that's enough for now," or "let me email you this one last article"), or physical (closing your browser window, looking at your watch, gathering materials on your desk, even starting to pack your bag). However, just as individuals with ASD often do not project social cues of their own, they also often do not pick up on them when exhibited by others. You cannot just hint that the session is over; you need to use clear language to express it. We suggest what we call the "kind, but direct" approach. Here are a couple of examples:

Situation: The student wants to chat, but someone else needs help.

Response: "I'm really enjoying our discussion, but others are waiting. I'm going to have to ask you to go now so that I can help the next person."

Situation: You are working with a student in your office and have gone past the appointment time.

Response: "I'm afraid I am out of time. You should go and work on [whatever the next step is] now. If you need more help later, you can set up another appointment."

You may notice that those suggestions are a little, well, blunt. This is where the *kind* of "kind, but direct" comes in. Your demeanor and tone should remain pleasant and friendly, even as what you say is very frank and specific. The *kind* part lets the student know that you are not angry and he or she has not done anything wrong. Still, this is not always a comfortable thing to do. Most librarians we know are very nice people who go out of their way to make others comfortable. The last thing we want to do is embarrass or offend anyone. However, our local expert has emphasized again and again that straightforward speaking is not only what students with ASD *need* but what they *want* (Müller et al. 2003). College students with ASD are aware that they sometimes miss the social cues and unwritten rules that neurotypical people operate under. They want to follow the rules and appreciate when others use straightforward language to explain how things work.

Because of difficulties with handling social situations, once a connection has been made, students with ASD may tend to seek help from the same librarian. For instance, one of the authors, Kerry, came to our university from a local community college. That same semester, a student with ASD with whom she had worked at her previous college transferred to our university to complete his degree. He was thrilled to find Kerry there, and she immediately became "his librarian." Kerry very much enjoyed working with this student, but she also knew it would be better for him to extend himself and seek help from others. Even though she emphasized that the other librarians are just as nice and helpful as she, to our knowledge, he never approached another librarian at the research help desk. He always waited until Kerry was on duty or sought her out in her office. A couple of times, Kerry had to employ the "kind, but direct" strategy described above. In one case, the student walked into her office and immediately started to take off his backpack and settle into a chair. It simply did not cross his mind that she might be otherwise occupied. So, Kerry simply told him she was about to go to a meeting and was not free to help him. She pulled out her calendar and suggested a time later in the day when she would be free and asked if he could come back then. He happily accepted and returned later in the day.

The next strategy is one that we will be repeating in multiple chapters throughout this book. Please remember to keep your wording straightforward in another way, by avoiding nonliteral language such as figures of speech, irony, and sarcasm. These types of speech are cases when you are saying things that you do not mean literally. In the case of irony and sarcasm, you often actually mean something quite the opposite from what your words express. If the student does not pick up on the tone of your voice indicating that you are being ironic or sarcastic, which can be difficult for individuals with ASD, he or she may misinterpret what you are saying. Please do not take this to mean that individuals with autism do not have a sense of humor or that you cannot joke with them, because that is absolutely not the case! It is only these specific types of humor that they have trouble understanding. Research supports that individuals with ASD enjoy other kinds of humor, from silly slapstick to sophisticated wordplay (Lyons and Fitzgerald 2004). In fact, our local expert has confirmed that many of her students enjoy language-based humor, especially puns. She fondly recalls when the president of our university came to visit her program. The first student who introduced himself made a pun based on his major ("I'm a geology major, and it rocks"), prompting each of the other students to quickly come up with similar wordplay related to their majors.

Overall, when we have found ourselves working with students with ASD, we have not found the interactions to be more difficult than working with neurotypical students, just a bit different. It mostly requires being thoughtful about what you are saying and how you are saying it. We feel that the thought and effort we have put into communicating with students with ASD has had a positive impact on all of our research help interactions. It has encouraged us to use direct language and ask more questions across the board, resulting in more engaged and productive consultations.

BEYOND THE REFERENCE DESK

It may occasionally be necessary to address the behavior of a student with ASD in the library. We do not expect this to be a common occurrence. As mentioned in Chapter 1, one common characteristic of individuals with ASD is they tend to be rule followers (Gobbo and Shmulsky 2014). In fact, they are much more likely to be irritated by another person breaking the rules! So, if they are breaking a rule, one of two things is probably occurring. One, they are not aware of the rule. This is especially true when one is talking about breaking an unwritten rule of social behavior. Two, the individual has become overwhelmed by external stimuli (noise, light, pattern, smell) because they are in a new space/situation, or because of stress. This can then result in the student not being able to consciously recall the appropriate rules for the situation. The student may start talking to themselves or someone else too loudly for a quiet area or may cut the line at the circulation desk. The "kind, but direct" approach should also be applied here. Kind, because the behavior is probably unintentional and you do not want to embarrass the student, only change the behavior. Direct, because they need to be taught or reminded of the rule they should be following—correct behavior for the situation. Ideally, if time and circumstances allow, contextualize the rule for the student. Provide the rule, the reasons for the rule, and if there are exceptions to the rule. It would also be helpful to provide contexts in which it would be okay to bend or break the rule. Understanding the nature and the purpose of the rule will not only help the student follow the rule but also help them manage potential anxiety if they see others breaking the rule.

You may also see students exhibiting repetitive behaviors (described in more detail in Chapter 2). Again, these sorts of behaviors are normal for individuals with ASD and are a way of coping with overstimulation and/or stress. As much as possible, the behavior should simply be ignored and the student left alone. They are using this behavior to try to calm down or regain their focus. Only if there is a situation where the behavior is interfering with the ability of other students to work (say, making noise in a quiet area), should it be addressed. Again, employ "kind, but direct", though in this case we would also inquire if there was anything we could help with. For instance, the student could be directed to an area where more noise is allowed if they want to talk or a quiet study room if it is too noisy for them. This is a particular area where librarians may need to advocate for students with ASD. If other staff or patrons are commenting or complaining about a student exhibiting a repetitive behavior, this is an excellent opportunity to educate them about what it is and why it happens.

If you are reading this book, you probably are, or hope to become, the point person in your own library for working with students with ASD. So, what can you do to help other librarians, staff, and student workers who will be encountering students with autism?

- If you have an official program on campus, ask if someone can give a presentation for those who work at service points in the library, or provide basic handouts. This is always our top choice because the staff is being trained by an expert, and it is an easy way to hit the majority of them at once.

- Provide some brief materials that could be read quickly (we suggest a couple of short articles at the end of the chapter) and also provide a sample fact sheet about autism (Appendix A). Although it is possible to find similar fact sheets on the web, we find that most of them are too broad. They often address the characteristics and behaviors that exist across the entire spectrum, which may not apply to adult college students with ASD.

- If time allows, consider putting together a folder or binder with tips and worksheets that can be kept at the reference desk or other service points.

EXECUTIVE FUNCTIONING

In Chapter 1, we extensively discussed executive functioning and how it impacts students' transitions to college. Now we are going to approach it specifically from the standpoint of students working on research assignments. To recap, executive functioning is a set of processes that are needed for individuals to be successful at *flexible, goal-oriented behavior*. This includes several skills that are extremely important to the research process:

- Planning, organization, and time management
- Mental flexibility
- Attention control/focus

Not only do executive functioning skills affect students' ability to manage a complex and variable college schedule in general, it can specifically cause difficulties in handling complex, multistep projects. The following description of how executive functioning impacts college-level assignments comes from an article on faculty experiences with students with ASD:

> A student who must complete a class assignment needs to plan or envision when and how to get things done and predict and locate the necessary materials. The student must activate or find a way to get started, monitor progress, and notice when things have gotten off track, either conceptually or in terms of attention; finally, the student must successfully shift back to goal-directed work, in this case, completion of the assignment at hand. All of these functions are critical to work completion, but none is about the content of the assignment per se [. . .]. (Gobbo and Shmulsky 2014)

The class assignment described above is not even necessarily a research paper, which is often one of the most complex projects that college students work on. A research paper is comprised of multiple steps [topic development, research, writing (including incorporating sources), editing, etc.]. Breaking down this type of large assignment can pose difficulties (Schindler et al. 2015). Those multiple steps must be completed over an extended period of time (usually from a few weeks to an entire semester). This requires not only a great deal of organization and time management but also the ability to shift focus as steps are completed and then as new steps begin. There may even be gaps of time between steps, forcing students to work on a project, set it aside, then return to it again. This requires the ability to regain focus. Within this larger writing project we find the research process, which is itself a multistep and complex process necessitating planning and time management. While researching, students must not only identify the proper research tools, develop successful searches, evaluate sources, and organize those sources for use, but they must also be able to adapt or develop new strategies if their first attempts are not successful. This need to adapt can be very problematic for students with ASD (Schindler et al. 2015). This demands a great deal of mental flexibility, especially as research does not always proceed in a series of discrete steps that follow a strict order (in other words, research is messy). Sometimes students have to go back a step in the process (e.g., adjust the thesis or develop new search terms) or move sideways (e.g., try a different database or source type) before they can move forward again. Indeed, the Framework for Information Literacy for Higher Education emphasizes this need for mental flexibility, especially in the dispositions of several frames.

ACRL FRAMEWORK FOR INFORMATION LITERACY FOR HIGHER EDUCATION DISPOSITIONS EMPHASIZING MENTAL FLEXIBILITY

Authority Is Constructed and Contextual

- Develop and maintain an open mind when encountering varied and sometimes conflicting perspectives

Research as Inquiry

- Consider research as open-ended exploration and engagement with information.
- Maintain an open mind and a critical stance.
- Value persistence, adaptability, and flexibility, and recognize that ambiguity can benefit the research process.
- Seek multiple perspectives during information gathering and assessment.

Searching as Strategic Exploration

- Exhibit mental flexibility and creativity.
- Understand that first attempts at searching do not always produce adequate results.
- Persist in the face of search challenges, and know when they have enough information to complete the information task. (Association of College & Research Libraries 2015)

As described above, none of this has anything to do with a student's intelligence, understanding of the content, or even the ability to write. Yet those executive functioning skills have a huge impact on a student's success in the research and research writing process. As librarians we even see neurotypical students struggle with this on a regular basis. The student who visits the reference desk asking for help finding sources the night before the paper is due is a common anecdote for a reason. For students with ASD, however, this is not a simple matter of having procrastinated about doing an unpleasant task; they actually have challenges that make organizing and completing this type of work difficult.

STUDENT VOICES

I had to do a research paper in my first year. My experience with it was horrible. It was a very stressful assignment and not my forte, and it was worth a large percentage of my grade. I was able to go to the writing center for help, in which they edited and provided good feedback on strengths and what I needed to improve.—**Zach G.**

SPECIFIC STRATEGIES

Below are some strategies for working with students with ASD in a research help situation. Some are techniques that you can implement in a reference desk/walk-up situation. Those are situations where you often will not know if a student has ASD, though you may suspect based on the social interaction as described above and in Chapter 1. Fortunately, we think a lot of the strategies discussed below are widely applicable to any student who is struggling with research, so they may still be quite useful for almost any student. Other strategies described below are things that can only be reasonably implemented if either (a) you know the student has ASD, or (b) it is a situation where you work with the same student repeatedly, such as being embedded into a class or serving as the subject specialist for the student's major.

Ask Concrete Questions

This is closely related to the more general approach of asking *more* questions discussed above under research help as a social interaction. Here we want to emphasize that it is helpful as much as possible to ask very specific, rather than open-ended questions. For instance,

Open-ended

What do you need?

Concrete

Tell me about the assignment you are working on.

Open-ended

What types of sources do you want?

Concrete

What type of sources does your professor require?

Do you need scholarly journal articles?

Can we take a look at the assignment prompt and see exactly what your professor says about sources?

This is another example of a technique that we have employed more broadly to our reference work. Any time a student seems uncertain or lost, a specific question can help get them back on track.

Use Visuals When Possible

Many individuals with ASD are strong visual learners or have difficulty with auditory learning (Zager et al. 2013). Graphic organizers are frequently cited as a helpful way for students with ASD to organize their thoughts, including specifically as part of the writing process (Jackson, Duffy et al. 2018; Meeks and Geither 2014a). If a student is still developing a topic, consider taking a few minutes to make a *concept map* with them, as this will allow them to visualize the connections between the main topic and subtopics and see how to connect search terms. Some other specific types of graphic organizers that might apply to the research process are storyboards and fact sheets. *Storyboarding* (taken from movie design) is similar to concept mapping but with an emphasis on sequence—how each idea will lead to the next (Meeks and Geither 2014b). It would be most applicable for students who have already done some research and are trying to organize what they have into a logical order in preparation for writing. *Fact sheets* are organizers where students use lists to organize pieces of information into groups or larger concepts (Meeks and Geither 2014a). These fact sheets can then potentially be developed into a fuller outline before writing. If the student also records the source information with each "fact," the fact sheet would also serve as a way to manage sources and could be developed into a Works Cited page later in the process.

Any of these approaches could be especially helpful for students with ASD for another reason, as well. Individuals with autism may tend to focus on smaller details and have difficulty seeing the big picture (a concept known as weak central coherence) (Gobbo and Shmulsky 2014; Hill 2004; Tops et al. 2017; Zager et al. 2013). In other words, they are often better at seeing the parts of something than the whole. In the context of the research process, this might mean that while a student has gathered research and is a master of all the facts, he or she still might struggle with organizing those facts into themes. The various techniques above can support this aspect of the research/writing process. Each helps students to see how parts of the topic or pieces of information from different sources fit together. This helps the main arguments and themes emerge, while also revealing what information or arguments are more tangential and should be eliminated.

Another option to help students with ASD organize the research process is simply to employ worksheets, such as you or a classroom professor would use during library instruction. Worksheets help divide the process into a series of manageable concrete tasks, like developing a topic, creating search terms, and selecting possible databases. No need to reinvent the wheel here; you can simply modify any worksheets already developed for classes as needed and keep some copies at hand in your office or reference desk. Finally, take time to show the students online research guides, videos, and tutorials that your library has created. This gives them visual materials that they can return to later and go through at their own pace.

Take Notes for Them

When our local expert suggested this, we were a bit taken aback. Taking notes for a student seemed odd. Sure, we had jotted down call numbers or names of databases or some good search terms for students, but never much beyond that. There are two separate factors related to ASD at play here. The first factor is that individuals with ASD often have problems with fine motor skills, which can lead to poor handwriting (Asaro-Saddler 2016; Kushki, Chau, and Anagnostou 2011). This can not only make taking notes laborious but interferes with thought transfer—in other words, the student understands what is said but cannot successfully transfer those ideas onto paper (Asaro-Saddler 2016). The second factor is potential problems with executive functioning, particularly multitasking/mental flexibility. Not everyone can take notes and actually absorb the content simultaneously. Problems taking notes are not limited to just individuals with ASD. Permission to record lectures or having a note taker in class is a common accommodation made available to support students with a number of physical and learning disabilities, including those with ASD (Sarrett 2017). However, these same students are not going to come to the reference desk or research appointment with a note taker in tow. Just as in the classroom, they are being put in a situation where they need to learn complex materials with multiple steps and would benefit from having notes to review later. As long as writing down some notes is not a great inconvenience for the librarian, why not do so? It may have a great impact on the student's ability to learn what you showed him or her. If you do not want to handwrite notes, consider opening a doc and typing as you go. Another option would be to print screen shots that show various steps in the process—especially where a lot is done on a single screen, like when searching a database. We have even had students take pictures of a screen with their phones.

Modeling

Modeling (either in person or using video) is a widely used strategy for teaching individuals developed in the field of applied behavior analysis (Cooper, Heron, and Heward 2007; Plavnick and Hume 2014). It is considered an established method for teaching specific behaviors (especially social or life skills) to children and adolescents with ASD (National Autism Center 2009, 2015) but can be applied to other contexts. Modeling allows the student to try out the behavior themselves after watching someone else doing it, increasing the likelihood it will be remembered. Because it is such a commonly used technique, it is an approach than many students with ASD (if diagnosed as children) are likely to feel very comfortable with. At the reference desk, modeling might simply involve allowing time for the student to follow your steps. You would show the step on your computer, and then the student could copy the step on their own laptop. In a situation where you were working with a student on more than one occasion, the modeling process could be more involved. Our local expert, Cherie Fishbaugh, suggests using three steps. The first time a librarian worked with the student, they would show the process with the student mostly observing. If a worksheet was involved, the librarian would be the one filling out the worksheet. The next time the librarian worked with the student, they would have the student take the lead but be very involved in providing guidance and correcting mistakes. The third time, the student would attempt to do the work himself or herself, and the librarian would review it after and offer suggestions if the student needed additional help.

Help Students Scaffold the Research Process

Rachel works with the English Studies department at our university, especially the composition program. Most of the faculty in that program do an outstanding job of breaking down the research and writing process into steps and building multiple due dates into the schedule (tentative topics due, then library instruction, a scheduled research day, annotated bibliography due, etc.). Dividing a long process into individual chunks is especially useful to those who face challenges with executive functioning (Burgstahler and Russo-Gleicher 2015; Meeks and Geither 2014a); however, not all professors do this. We have certainly also seen plenty of large research assignments, especially for upper-level undergraduate or graduate courses, that do not do this. The professor hands out an assignment prompt near the beginning of the semester, with a due date at the end and not a single milepost in the middle. This can lead to exactly the sort of situation described above, where a student who is entirely capable of understanding the materials and writing about it nevertheless struggles because of the problems managing the complicated process of the assignment.

This is another area where librarians could provide support. Granted, this is not a question a librarian is likely to hear at the reference desk, since a student is most likely to ask only for help with finding sources. But there are situations where this may come up—the librarian is embedded in a class, teaching a credit-bearing course, or serves as a liaison to their college's autism support program. The process is relatively straightforward. The librarian just needs to have a copy of the assignment and the course schedule. Once armed with the details of the assignment and the due date, the librarian can talk to the student about ways to break the assignment into smaller chunks, then working backward from the final due date, give each of these "mini assignments" its own due date.

Of course, such a schedule would be adjusted based on the assignment, how much time was available, and what steps make sense to that particular

SAMPLE RESEARCH PAPER SCHEDULE

Today's date: **February 16**
Final paper due: **May 10**

- Select tentative topic **(February 20).**
- Make a concept map and select search terms **(February 26).**
- Complete first-round research **(March 5).**
- Finish reading all sources found; make an initial fact sheet **(March 19).**
- Look for any more needed sources. If help needed, set up appointment with librarian **(March 26).**
- Finish fact sheet and turn it into an outline **(April 5).**
- Complete first draft **(April 23).**
- Take first draft to writing center **(April 30).**
- Final paper due **(May 10).**

student. In some cases, the students may want to break down the self-imposed assignments into even smaller segments that can be tackled in "20-minute mini sessions," which allows them to keep their focus on a small task and feel a sense of accomplishment when it is completed and crossed off the list (Meeks and Geither 2014a).

Try to Not Cover Everything at Once

Covering too much material is certainly a personal challenge of Rachel (one of the authors), both in instruction sessions and when providing research help. The urge to cover everything a student could possibly need in one session or appointment can be very strong, as we want to give the student every potential tool that will help them succeed. But this approach can backfire with students with ASD, who may have more trouble than neurotypical students absorbing large amounts of information presented at once, especially if that information is being presented verbally (LeGary 2017; Zager et al. 2013). Instead of helping them succeed, you may in fact be overwhelming them to the point that they absorb very little of what you have been trying to teach them. A better approach is to help them learn what they need for the work at hand, then encourage them to return once they have completed that step for more help. This is another case where we have found that learning about and working with students with ASD has informed and changed our practice in general. Now that Rachel realizes that an overabundance of information can hurt rather than help certain students, she finds it much easier to monitor herself and carefully consider when she should provide more information and when she should stop.

TIPS FROM OUR EXPERT

Cherie Fishbaugh, MA, BCBA, BS-L (PA)

When assisting a student with a research paper/project, it is important to remember our student's strengths and areas of need. The majority of our students on the spectrum are visual learners and do best with consistency; however, taking notes and then applying procedures may be difficult. To better assist our students, use best practices such as:

- Provide visual aids including lists, graphic organizers, concept maps/ diagrams, and/or framed outlines.

- Provide a written task analysis of steps to complete a research paper/ project. This will also assist staff in being consistent when guiding the student through the process.

- Be consistent! If staff are assisting using different templates or procedures, this can lead to great frustration for the student. Having a binder/ resource for staff to refer to for assisting with consistency is highly recommended.

- Provide several examples and/or templates, including a list of common errors.

- When talking to the student, check for clarification by having them repeat back what they need to do.

- Provide clear and concise instruction. Long, multiple-step instructions can be difficult; break them down into smaller instructions.

- If needed, provide modeling for the student. Then have the student complete step with you, and eventually independently. Explicitly teaching through the "I do it, We do it, You do it" model is an effective teaching strategy.

- Lastly, remain calm. The student may get overwhelmed and frustrated. By remaining calm and breaking down the task at hand, it will assist the student in staying calm. It may be necessary to have the student complete one step of the process with instructions to come back for support to move on to step two.

Make a Clear End to the Reference Interview

This serves two purposes. The first is to help the student by clearly outlining the next step(s) that the student should take. If the student has problems with planning and time management, the next step might not be obvious to him or her! Along with the next step, let them know what they can do if they need more help. Here are a couple of examples:

> Since you have your laptop, why don't you set up [point out a good area] and try your topic in [database you just showed them]. After that, if you still are not sure if it is a good topic, discuss it with your professor.

> I think we have a good start here. I emailed you several articles. Why don't you go now and get this print book from the shelf and start reading some of the sources we found. If you need more help later, you can [come back to the reference desk again/set up another appointment with me].

The second purpose is to make a clear ending to the current help session. Telling a student that they should go and work on something else is a fairly direct way to signal the end, yet perhaps a little less blunt than some of the examples given at the beginning of the chapter.

Take Time to Explain Library Systems

We mentioned in Chapter 1 that while ASD is defined medically by diagnostic criteria that focus on limitations in certain areas, there is also more and more evidence for a specific strength profile for those with ASD. One of the strengths is that many with ASD enjoy a systemizing approach—that is, they like "activities that involve analyzing, constructing, or controlling a system. A system is defined as something that follows repeated, lawful patterns" (Kirchner and Dziobek 2014). Systems play a crucial role in libraries as a whole and thus the research process. The idea of explaining library systems in reference/instruction was first mentioned in an article by Remy and Seaman (2014) specifically in the context of explaining how classification systems work (call number and subject headings). But we think this can be expanded to include library databases as well, with their search algorithms and limiters. Certain students with ASD might really appreciate knowing how much control they can have over their search process by employing some of these features. Frankly, we think it would be great to work with some students who actually find proximity searching or using the thesaurus exciting!

Show Options for Organizing Research Materials

As we discussed, executive functioning impacts organization. Although we tend to focus on helping students find and evaluate sources, they also need to organize them for later use. Showing students on the spectrum ways to store and cite materials may be even more important than for neurotypical students. Going back to our tip of not showing everything—do not show them every bibliographic management tool out there! Pick one or two options to demonstrate based on what they have done in the past, which library tools they will be using, and the scope of the project at hand. If possible, take the time to have them set up an account (if required) or practice using the tool a time or two.

Move Away from the Desk If Needed

Chapter 2 discussed in detail how students with ASD may react to environmental stimuli. It may be that your own reference desk area may have factors (lighting, busy location, noise, etc.) that make it an uncomfortable place for a student with sensitivities. If this is the case, try moving away from the desk to a more comfortable situation (Cherney 2017). If the student has a laptop, you could leave the desk altogether to take the student to a more conducive location—perhaps one where they could continue working once you get them started. If that is not an option, see if another librarian is free to work with the student in his or her office, where there is more control over certain aspects of the environment, or set up an appointment to work in your office later.

Advertise Chat and Email Options

This suggestion circles back around to where we began—research assistance as a social interaction. Many students with ASD prefer online interactions to in-person ones (Sarrett 2017). Some may be more likely to seek help if they can do so electronically instead of in-person. If your campus has an official support program for students with ASD, that would be the perfect venue to advertise chat and/or email reference services. If not, reaching out to your office of services for students with disabilities would be the best bet.

CONCLUSION

What we hope you take away from this chapter is that you do not have to make radical changes in order to provide good research assistance to students with ASD. We do not think that any of the suggestions above are particularly revolutionary. With the possible exceptions of taking notes for students and helping scaffold research assignments, many of the strategies we introduced are variations of strategies that we already employ in certain circumstances (though perhaps with a tweak) and could serve as a list of best practices for reference services more generally. Once an experienced librarian is aware of the basic characteristics of ASD and how they might impact research, it is not too difficult to make some simple adjustments to tailor the experience for the needs of autistic students.

RECOMMENDED READING

Meeks, Lisa, and Elise Geither. 2014. *Helping Students with Autism Spectrum Disorder Express Their Thoughts and Knowledge in Writing Tips and Exercises for Developing Writing Skills.* London: Jessica Kingsley.

> Although the focus of the book is writing, rather than researching, many of both the potential problems and strategies provided can be transferred to the latter. Chapter 3 (Executive Functioning) and Chapter 10 (Extended Writing Project) are extremely short, yet provide a good introduction to the issues.

Remy, Charlie, and Priscilla Seaman. 2014. "Evolving from Disability to Diversity: How to Better Serve High-Functioning Autistic Students." *Reference & User Services Quarterly* 54, no. 1: 24–28. https://journals.ala.org/rusq/article/download/3968/4454.

> This article is very short but covers a lot of territory in just over four pages, touching on different models for defining disability, basic characteristics of ASD, and some tips for reference, instruction, and outreach. That makes it an ideal article to share with other librarians or staff who may work with students at service points.

FOUR

Library Instruction

A chapter on providing instruction for college students with ASD is made tricky by the fact that academic librarians conduct many different types of instruction. Some librarians exclusively do "one shots," where a class comes to the library for instruction maybe once or twice during the semester. On the other hand, some librarians are responsible for teaching full semester-length courses dedicated to information literacy. Yet other librarians teach mainly online, which can also take a variety of implementations—synchronous session, embedded in the course management system, or developing online tutorials. The strategies that a librarian can actually employ to support students with ASD vary greatly depending on the exact circumstances. Therefore, we will be dividing this chapter into three sections. The first will be dedicated to those teaching one-shot instruction. This allows us to begin by addressing the more limited number of strategies that apply to that very specific context. We will then expand on those strategies in the second section addressing credit-bearing classes. Finally, a short third section will look at online instruction.

ACADEMIC STRENGTHS AND WEAKNESSES OF STUDENTS WITH ASD

The diagnostic criteria of ASD and how they apply to college students have been covered in previous chapters. In this chapter, we will consider how those criteria might specifically affect teaching and learning during library-related instruction.

- **Social and Communication Issues:** Communication was addressed in both Chapters 1 (general) and 3 (specific to research assistance). Communication difficulties can also affect how students with ASD interact with both the classroom instructor and fellow students. It can especially impact any type of group work or project.

- **Executive Functioning and Information Processing:** Executive functioning was addressed in detail in Chapter 3, where we discussed how it might impact the research process. In this chapter, we will focus on strategies that support students who may have executive functioning and information processing difficulties inside and outside of the classroom.

- **Environmental Sensitivities:** Chapter 2 focused on sensitivities and how they might affect a student within the physical library. This chapter will look at the same issues, but from the perspective of the classroom environment.

Let us not forget that students with ASD also have a number of academic strengths. For example, in a study that identified "signature strengths" of individuals with autism, three of the top five were categorized as intellectual strengths. These were open-mindedness, love of learning, and creativity (Kirchner, Ruch, and Dziobek 2016). The article's authors define open-minded people as those who "examine aspects from all sides, weigh the pros and cons carefully and do not jump to conclusions impulsively." This is a valuable attribute not only for any class with an emphasis on critical thinking but especially for classes involving a research project. Creative individuals are more likely to be original thinkers, and the advantage of love of learning as a trait in college students is rather obvious! A survey of faculty members who had worked with college students adds three more strengths to this profile: passionate interests, adherence to rules, and having a desire to be right (Gobbo and Shmulsky 2014). Being passionate about interests means students may be willing to put extra time and energy into topics and projects that intrigue them. This will in turn engage them in important college-level skills like reading, research, and writing. Being strict rule followers means that students with ASD will do their best to follow classroom rules, procedures, and due dates. The final strength, a desire to be right, does not initially sound like a particularly positive trait, because it can be associated with aggressiveness or argumentativeness. However, this is not what the authors of the study meant. Instead, they mean that because students with ASD want to be correct and not get things wrong, they are likely to pay attention to detail, ask for clarification, and gather a lot of knowledge on a subject. Another point made in the same report is that, while studies have shown that those with autism may have trouble with understanding the "big picture" (idea of central coherence), the flip side is that they are very good with details and pieces (focus on the trees rather than the forest). This is a trait that we will revisit in Chapter 5 on employment.

These academic traits really reinforce the concept of neurodiversity that we discussed in the introduction to this book. In many cases, individuals with ASD simply think and approach problems *differently* than neurotypical individuals. In some cases, this will make it hard for them to fit into traditional college classrooms, but in other cases these differences will help them stand out and shine as students. The next step is to explore ways that we as instructors can help them be as successful as possible in the college environment.

UNIVERSAL DESIGN FOR INSTRUCTION

In Chapter 2, we introduced the concept of Universal Design (UD) as a way to make spaces and objects more accessible and usable for a wide range of people. Not long after the establishment of Universal Design, scholars began applying its concepts to education. Scholars at the Center on Applied Special Technology (CAST) developed Universal Design for Learning (CAST 2018). Based on the overarching concept of Universal Design, they designed three broad principles for making learning flexible and accessible to as many individuals as possible. These principles include educators providing:

* Multiple means of engagement.

* Multiple means of representation.

* Multiple means of action and engagement. (Meyer, Rose, and Gordon 2014)

Universal Design for Learning (UDL) has been widely adopted in K–12 education. Following Universal Design for Learning, several groups of scholars have worked to provide guidance for implementing UD principles to postsecondary education. A number of different frameworks have been made to expand on UD and UDL and help college educators apply their main tenets (Parker 2012). For simplicity, we have selected just one of those frameworks as our model for library instruction: Universal Design for Instruction (UDI).

UDI was developed by scholars at the University of Connecticut (Scott, McGuire, and Shaw 2003). They incorporated concepts from both UD and UDL, as well as the Seven Principles of Good Practice in Undergraduate Education (Chickering and Gamson 1987). The final product involved the adaptation of the original seven principles of UD, plus the addition of two more, to meet the needs of instruction at the college level.

Principles of Universal Design for Instruction

1. Equitable use
2. Flexibility in use
3. Simple and intuitive instruction
4. Perceptible information
5. Tolerance for error
6. Low physical effort
7. Size and space for approach and use
8. A community of learners
9. Instructional climate (Scott, McGuire, and Shaw 2003)

The principles of UDI are meant to help encourage educators (including librarians) to consider and take into account the various abilities and disabilities their students might have when designing course material. When applied to instruction, the principle of *equitable use* means that all students should be able to access and use all the materials. Common examples would be the use of closed captioning on videos to make them accessible to those with a hearing impairment or adding a detailed caption to an image for those with a visual impairment. *Flexibility in use* for instruction addresses not only the diverse abilities of students but also diverse learning styles. Providing a variety of instruction methods and assignments can allow each student in the class opportunities to learn and demonstrate their knowledge in ways that suit them. The unique strength and weakness profiles of students with ASD make this a very important principle to employ.

The principle of *simple and intuitive instruction* demands that instruction be delivered in a "straightforward and predictable manner." Given that many individuals with autism prefer a great deal of structure and predictability in all aspects of their lives, this principle is one of the most important to keep in mind when working with students on the spectrum. The same can be said of Principle 5, *tolerance for error,* which includes a focus on "learning pace" (Scott, McGuire, and Shaw 2003). We mentioned in Chapter 3 that students with ASD may need more time to process information (especially when presented verbally) than neurotypical students, so pacing can be an important issue for them.

Principles 8 and 9 (*a community of learners* and *instructional climate*) were the two principles added by the creators of UDI (Scott, McGuire, and Shaw 2003). They are very important to consider when working with students with ASD, because of the social and communication challenges associated with autism. Both principles deal with the classroom/learning environment, with *a community of learners* focusing on encouraging positive communication and *instructional climate* focusing on making the learning environment as welcoming and inclusive as possible.

The final three principles are the ones we found to be the least relevant to students with ASD, because their application is primarily for individuals with physical disabilities (though we did provide at least one strategy that relates to each). *Perceptible information* focuses on providing information in a way so that it can be absorbed and understood by everyone. *Low physical effort* emphasizes eliminating any unnecessary tasks that require physical effort. *Size and space for approach and use* asks the teacher to consider if the instruction space (either physical or online) could be adapted to make it more accessible by all.

Every strategy we will discuss throughout this chapter can be tied back to these principles of UDI. We will show this connection by including the related UDI principle after each strategy. Some strategies actually align with more than one principle. In this case, we have decided to align the strategy to the principle that we think makes the most sense in the context of working with students with ASD. For instance, providing notes has been listed by other authors as a technique under Principle 1: Equitable use (Scott, McGuire, and Shaw 2003). However, because note taking can be difficult for students with ASD partially because of fine motor skills, we aligned it with Principle 6: Low physical effort.

Just as Universal Design tries to make the physical world as accessible as possible for everyone, Universal Design for Instruction tries to make college education as accessible as possible from the beginning. The current model for supporting students with any disability at the university level is driven by the language of the Americans with Disabilities Act (ADA). It states that colleges must provide accommodations to students with documented disabilities. For instance, in Chapter 3 we discussed that a common college classroom accommodation (for a number of disabilities) is recording a lecture or having a note taker in class. There are a couple of major downsides to this current system. The first is that it puts the onus on the individual student to seek out the accommodations they need each semester with each professor—this could be dozens of classes over a college career. The second is that the professors must respond to any requests for accommodations presented in the first week of class. This occurs long after they have developed the course materials and syllabus (Scott, McGuire, and Shaw 2003). UDI, on the other hand, starts from the premise of the professor doing as much as possible to make the course accessible to all enrolled students from the onset of course design. This approach serves two good purposes. First, in some cases, it may mean students with documented disabilities do not need to seek special accommodations. Second, as we already discussed, many other students in class may also benefit from UDI principles incorporated into the course's design. Let us go back to the accommodation of a note taker in class. What if the professor provided class notes for lectures instead? In the case of students with ASD, it is beneficial for them because of potential difficulties with taking notes, information processing, and distractions in the physical environment. However, posting class notes may also support ESL students, hearing impaired students who missed something said in lecture, a student who missed class because of illness, or even a student who was hesitant to ask the professor to repeat or clarify something.

The strategies that we will discuss below either come directly from the UDI literature or can be aligned with it. We do, however, need to add one caveat—not every technique suggested for UDI is going to be a great technique for students with ASD. One example is the use of clickers (or other student response programs) in the classroom. Some scholars have suggested using them as a UDI strategy for engaging students in the classroom, especially in large lectures (Izzo and Bauer 2015; Parker 2012). However, given that those with ASD may have trouble shifting their focus or may need more time to process information, being forced to respond to timed questions at intervals during a class may be distracting rather than beneficial. There are also potential issues with group work, another commonly suggested strategy, which we will address in more detail later in the chapter. Remember that the idea of UDI is that by employing various teaching methods, each student will hopefully have one or more methods that work well for their learning style—*not* that every method is great for every student.

First, one general tip. Save yourself time and energy by tapping into the knowledge of professionals if they are available! Instructional designers may have a background in UD/UDI, many creative ideas, and possibly even staff who have time to take on bigger projects than you could on your own. Some larger academic libraries may even have an instructional design expert on staff. If not, check to see if your college or university employs instructional designers on campus—perhaps through an office to support teaching excellence or distance education.

ONE-SHOT INSTRUCTION

Our university libraries have a strong one-shot instruction program, so this is a type of teaching that is near and dear to our hearts. We are also well aware of the limitations it places on the librarian instructor. Two of these limitations (time and the unknown) are very familiar but take on an extra layer of consideration when thinking about teaching students with ASD.

Time is a major consideration for those teaching one-shot sessions—not only class time but also preparation time. Limited class time versus the amount of material you want to cover is *always* an issue. However, as already introduced in Chapter 3, pacing is a specific issue for students with ASD, who may need more time to absorb information, especially in a new and unfamiliar environment. Having enough prep time is also frequently a challenge as most librarians have to balance teaching with plenty of other responsibilities. Even though many of the strategies we will discuss below are not particularly time intensive to incorporate, it will still take some extra time to think about your class, the potential strategies you want to implement, and then make the changes. In some cases, all this work may be for a class you only teach once or twice a year!

The other factor that constantly impacts one-shot sessions is "the unknown". What librarian has not faced a computer crashing or a database not working or the projector suddenly breaking down? Even worse is when the professor is unexpectedly absent or has fallen behind in their teaching and their students are not where you thought they would be. Having students with ASD in your class is another potential unknown factor. Unlike the classroom professor, who will be made aware of at least some special needs of students through requests for accommodations in the first week of class, a librarian almost always walks into a session with no idea of who the students are or their needs. Between themselves, the two authors of this book have taught around 1,500 library sessions over the course of their careers. Although we have both occasionally had a professor mention issues with a particular section, only once has a professor informed either one of us about the learning needs or required accommodations for a particular student. It can be hard to make changes to your instruction based on the likelihood that you might have a student with ASD in your sessions, but that is where UDI as a concept is so beneficial. Many of the strategies we discuss below, while selected specifically to support students with ASD, also have much wider applicability.

What You May Notice

If you have a student with ASD in a one-shot session, you may not notice at all. If you do, it will almost certainly be social/communication or behavioral aspects that come to your attention. We discussed environmental sensitivities in great detail in Chapter 2 and in passing in Chapter 3. For some students with ASD, this may present a significant challenge, especially if the class has come to a classroom in the library. In their regular classroom, a student may have already identified a space to sit that suits them best depending on their own needs. A library classroom is a brand new space to them that may present new challenges to which they have not had a chance to adjust. Please remember that something in the environment that might only be a slight annoyance to most neurotypical people may be an overwhelming distraction to someone with ASD who is hypersensitive. The hum the computers or monitors make, the texture of the seat fabric, the flicker of a fluorescent light, the pattern of the carpet, or many other environmental factors in a classroom may be problematic (Elwin et al. 2013; Robledo, Donnellan, and Strandt-Conroy 2012). Saying these stimuli annoy them is much too weak a term. A student with ASD may reach a point of sensory overload, where the stimuli are overwhelming their senses and causing significant stress to the point that they are unable to learn (Elwin et al. 2013). If this occurs, you may notice a couple of different types of behavior.

First, you may see students employing repetitive behaviors (also known as self-stimulatory behavior or, colloquially, a "stim") as a way of coping with the sensory overload. The use of repetitive behaviors is extremely common for those with ASD. The very best description we have found for what this type of behavior does is from an article by Tomlinson and Newman (2017), from the point of view of an individual with ASD.

> [I]f you notice a stim happening, we're just having trouble connecting to our thoughts probably due to a distraction in the environment. The stim kind of helps us disconnect to think because when we focus on the stim it helps block out the environment and lets us transition to thought.

Often a stim involves physical motion—finger tapping, touching objects, hand movements, rocking, etc.—but it can also be auditory. We had one student in our library who used a throat-clearing sound on a regular basis. The key point here is that students exhibiting repetitive behaviors are not trying to be rude or distract others. They are doing their best to engage and learn in what is for them a stressful environment. Please do not draw attention to the behavior unless it is absolutely necessary—that will only serve to embarrass the student. If it is becoming a distraction, we suggest looking for an opportunity to introduce a break from the current activity. For instance, give the class a few minutes to try out something you just taught or work on a handout. This will hopefully give the class professor or yourself an opportunity to check in with the student and see if something can be done to help or for the student to discreetly leave the classroom for a few minutes. Ideally, you would know of a quiet place near the classroom where you could direct a student who needs a break (Gobbo and Shmulsky 2012). Sometimes the sensory overload can become so overwhelming that the student may be forced to suddenly leave the room in the middle of class in order to escape the situation (Smith and Sharp 2013). There is nothing you can do at that point as a teacher other than hope they are able to calm down enough to return to class, and offer to work with them outside of class, if they miss a substantial portion of it.

The other situation that may arise with a student with ASD in a single session is his or her level of engagement—particularly too much engagement. We will discuss the flip side of this issue—lack of engagement, in the section on longer classes. Given how much librarians have to work to get students participating in a one-shot class, it can be hard to imagine a

SAMPLE SCENARIOS

Situation: Student is asking many questions. They may be off-topic or simply taking up too much class time.

Sample Response: That's a great question, but we don't have a lot of class time today and I'm falling behind. Please jot down any other questions and I'll be happy to answer them after class.

Situation: Student is jumping in and answering all questions.

Sample Response: I'm going to ask another question. This time I'd like to hear from someone who hasn't answered before. (Burgstahler and Russo-Gleicher 2015)

Then you simply have to follow through by being available for the student outside the class. This is hardly a hardship for most librarians—we enjoy talking to students about their research and their research topics!

case of too much engagement! We are always thrilled when a student asks a question, especially in an undergraduate session. Yet, if one student asks repeated questions or jumps in to answer every question that is posed by the instructor, there can be a negative impact on the class. It can not only frustrate other students in the class, but it can also throw off the pace of the class in a time-sensitive situation. If you have a student who is dominating the class discussion, we suggest the same "kind, but direct" approach that we introduced in Chapter 3. That is, your demeanor remains pleasant and friendly, even as your words need to be clear and direct (even a trifle blunt). You are not trying to call out the behavior or embarrass the student for talking too much but simply trying to stop the behavior. The student is not trying to be problematic. If anything, you should take it as a compliment, because they are finding the class topic engaging!

Strategies for One-Shot Sessions

Use Direct, Literal Language

This has also been addressed in both Chapter 1 and Chapter 3 but is important enough that it bears repeating. Individuals with ASD have trouble with nonliteral language (metaphors, unfamiliar figures of speech, idioms, irony, sarcasm, etc.) and may misinterpret it (Zager et al. 2013). This tip is actually a great example of the tenets of UDI. Although at first glance this may seem like an approach that benefits only students with ASD, it could also benefit students for whom English is a second language and may also struggle with the nonliteral.

Related UDI principle: Perceptible information

Provide Structure

Offering structure provides students who may have trouble processing information rapidly a framework for what will be happening in the session, making it easier for them to follow along. We will discuss this more below, as there are many more opportunities to provide structure in a full course than in a single session. However, even in a one-shot class, you can take just a couple of minutes at the beginning of the session to review your lesson plan both verbally and in print (see below) (Chodock and Dolinger 2009). Taking another minute or two to review key points or ask a couple of questions at the end would also help by reinforcing what you see as the most important content covered in the session.

Related UDI principle: Simple and intuitive instruction

Provide Backup

This is probably the single most essential suggestion we have for those teaching one-shot sessions. Often we can do very little to control our teaching environments. We must teach in the classroom space we are given. We have a certain amount of information that we really need to cover in a short amount of time. Those circumstances may not present an ideal learning environment for some students, including those with ASD. If we provide some sort of backup that a student can return to after the class is over, we are giving them a second chance to learn the material. For most professors the course management system (CMS) serves this purpose quite well (UDI Online Project 2009). For many libraries, software like LibGuides has really revolutionized what it is possible for librarians to create to support classes, especially because it allows us to reuse materials we or our colleagues have created for multiple classes. Whenever possible, an online research guide of some sort should be a librarian's top choice. Why online? Placing material online allows for the use of assistive technology, such as screen-reading software, as well as the incorporation of videos and tutorials that can help students by presenting the material in different ways (Izzo and Bauer 2015). If you cannot make an online guide, a print guide is still a viable option. Especially if the order of the handout follows the lecture, it can help students follow along or even help them take notes.

Related UDI principle: Tolerance for error

Post Class Notes

This is an approach that is mentioned both as a specific technique to support students with ASD (Burgstahler and Russo-Gleicher 2015; Zager et al. 2013) and as a general example of a UDI best practice (Scott, McGuire, and Shaw 2003). Posting notes for a one-shot class allows students to come back and review the information again later. In a full course, it also allows students to preview the material and print out the notes (or slides) to bring to class to assist in their own note taking. For a single session, the librarian could ask the course professor to post the notes to the CMS prior to the class. We admit that this is an example of a best practice that is not always particularly well adapted to the single session model. If it is the first time you have worked with a particular class, taking time to type up a class outline or build a PowerPoint (in addition to preparing for the class and making an online guide), may be more than you can accomplish. We suggest that you prioritize by first making notes for classes for which you teach multiple sections or teach year after year. If you normally make an outline or script as part of your class preparation, you can use these as a starting point by simply formalizing and elaborating on them a bit.

Related UDI principle: Low physical effort

Present Information Both Verbally and Visually

This is a general UDI principle that reflects both the needs of those with certain physical disabilities (sight or hearing impairment) and also various learning styles. It is also particularly beneficial for students with ASD who may have problems with auditory processing (Zager et al. 2013). Having visuals to support a lecture or discussion format can help those students stay on track. Visuals can take several different forms. One is to incorporate graphic images, videos, and even physical models into class lectures and discussions when possible (Shaw 2011). Another suggestion that is specific to library instruction is to make sure to print (avoid cursive, which is harder to read) all search terms on the board (Chodock and Dolinger 2009). This can also help those who are poor typists or spellers. Instructions for hands-on activities or discussion questions should also be provided in a print format in addition to verbally.

Earlier in the book, we discussed using worksheets to help students with ASD with the research process (Zager et al. 2013). The same advice applies equally here. Worksheets can help students with ASD not only by providing a way to learn visually but also by helping them organize their thoughts or information. Please refer back to Chapter 3 for some specific examples.

Related UDI principle: Equitable use

Teach Only Skills Related to the Assignment

This suggestion was taken from Chodock and Dolinger's (2009) excellent article on using UDI principles for teaching information literacy to students with various disabilities. Although they were not specifically looking at students with ASD, this tip does apply to them very well. In the last chapter on research assistance, we discussed how weaknesses with executive functioning and information processing can make it hard for those with ASD to process large amounts of information quickly (Zager et al. 2013). We realize that *not* providing as much information as you can squeeze into your session can be really hard for librarians. It certainly is for us! At our own university, because of the structure of some curriculums, some students may attend only a single library information literacy session during his or her entire college career, which only increases the urge to cover as much ground as possible. However, it is better that the students learn only a few things rather than that they learn nothing at all because we have taught an overwhelming amount of information!

If you are struggling with this, one way to approach it is to write yourself just a couple of learning outcomes for the session. Then, review your class plan. If there are things you are showing or discussing that do not contribute to those learning outcomes, consider cutting them from the lesson plan.

Remember that you can always include extra materials on your class guide or handout.

Related UDI principle: Simple and intuitive instruction

Make the Physical Environment Friendly

This can be a difficult strategy to implement, because many of us are stuck with the teaching space we have with little or no budget to make big changes. However, we can at least take a fresh look at our classrooms, trying to see them through the lens of someone with sensory issues. This will allow us to help a student with ASD find the best seat in class for their own needs (Gobbo and Shmulsky 2012). Try sitting in various parts of your classroom yourself. Is there a certain spot where the heating/AC vent blasts people? An area where the whine of the overhead projector is the loudest? Certain computers where the glare off the screen is especially bad? Then try to brainstorm simple fixes. Can unused equipment be turned off to avoid mechanical hums? Can furniture be rearranged to help give everyone a clear view of the instructor and board? Can the amount of fluorescent lighting used be reduced and any natural light be taken advantage of or softer incandescent or LED lighting introduced? Perhaps antiglare screens could be attached to monitors. If nothing else, you will be better prepared to help students with ASD (or any disability) find the best spot in the classroom for their learning. Of course, if you ever do have the opportunity to renovate your spaces, review Chapter 2 for more suggestions.

Related UDI principle: Size and space for approach and use

Provide a Break

Providing a break can allow an individual who is feeling overwhelmed either by the amount/speed of information being presented or by factors in the environment a chance to rest and regroup. If you are teaching a longer class, this could be an actual 10-minute break, allowing students to move around or leave the classroom (Burghstahler and Russo-Gleicher 2015). In a shorter class, consider providing a break from teacher-directed work, whether it is lecturing or group activities, to allow for self-directed work time. Chodock and Dolinger (2009) actually suggest that librarians try to leave one-third to one-half of their class time for students to work by themselves.

Related UDI principle: Tolerance for error

THOUGHTS FROM OUR EXPERT: WORKING WITH STUDENTS WITH ASD

Cherie Fishbaugh, MA, BCBA, BS-L (PA)

During lecture or class activities it is helpful to eliminate multitasking, by providing guided notes and/or stopping media presentations when discussing content. If able, teach concepts [in] different ways: verbal, visual, tangible, role playing, etc. Utilize the use of visual and assistive technologies such as the smart board. In addition, there are many other visual aids to use while teaching, including graphic organizers, charts, graphs, video demonstrations, concept maps/concept diagrams, framed outlines, structured worksheets, computer-based instruction, advanced organizers, and study guides.

FULL/CREDIT-BEARING COURSES

One of the things you may see if you teach a longer class, such as a credit-bearing course, is a request for accommodations. As mentioned above, accommodations are a part of the Americans with Disabilities Act. In order to qualify for accommodations, students must provide documentation of a disability to a campus's office for students with disabilities, which then creates a list of specific accommodations. Common accommodations for college students with ASD include extended time on tests, an alternative (distraction-free) testing space, use of a computer or technology supports (like a smart pen), and a note taker in class (Barnhill 2016; Sarrett 2017; Wolf, Brown, and Bork 2009). Others that have been reported, but less consistently, include recording lectures, being able to take a break from class, and extended due dates for assignments (Sarrett 2017).

As we discussed with one-shot sessions above, you may not know that you have a student in class with ASD. If they present you with accommodations, their paperwork will only state what accommodations are requested, not *why* they are needed. You will only know that if a student chooses to disclose, and students are certainly not required to do so. If a student does elect to disclose, we encourage you to offer to meet with him or her one-on-one so you can discuss that student's particular needs. If a student with ASD does not disclose, you may never even suspect unless you note awkward social/communication behavior or something stressful happens in class that leads to the student exhibiting disruptive behavior. Examples could be the student engaging in a repetitive behavior, raising his or her voice, or leaving the classroom. Our local expert, Cherie, tells us that in her experience, the most common cause of a student with ASD exhibiting disruptive behavior in class or in front of a professor is when the professor makes an unexpected change to the course (e.g., a change in the class schedule or an assignment).

THOUGHTS FROM OUR EXPERT: MEETING WITH STUDENTS WITH ASD

Cherie Fishbaugh, MA, BCBA, BS-L (PA)

When meeting with a student on the spectrum, keep in mind the following proactive strategies:

- Have consistent procedures for activities (office hours, grading, contacting).

- Make your intentions clear (What is the agenda? What is your role? How can you help?).

- Be concrete (I will get back to you versus I will call tomorrow between 1 and 3).

- Allow time for the student to collect their thoughts before anticipating an answer. Also allow the student to explain their interpretation of the assignment.

- Use clear and consistent facial expressions to match the meaning of your words. For instance, if you laugh or smile when stating that extra credit is not given in class, the student may interpret the laugh as a joke.

- Reduce background noise and chatter, especially if shared office space. Move to a quiet area free of others typing, talking, and/or visibly walking by.

- Promote self-advocacy.

- Provide direct feedback, stating explicitly what they need to improve.

- Set expectations (time limits, communication style, how to wait, how to approach etc.).

- Have a plan for continued communication. (Set aside time during your office hours for the student; continue to ask questions to assess student's progress and anxiety level.)

If a serious classroom disruption happens, and you either know or suspect that the student has ASD, we encourage you to contact your campus ASD program (if one exists) or the office of services for students with disabilities and seek support for working with the student to change unwelcome classroom behavior. However, it is important to also remember that ultimately, students with ASD do need to meet class expectations, including behavior standards. We want to provide supports that will help them succeed, but if a particular student continues to exhibit behaviors that disrupt class on a regular basis that impede other students' ability to learn even after intervention, you have the right to and should pursue whatever procedures your institution has in place regarding student conduct, just as you would with any student (Wolf, Brown, and Bork 2009).

Now, let us move on to some concrete strategies. Just a reminder—the strategies for one-shot sessions we discussed above can also be applied to a credit-bearing class. First, we will begin with approaches that have been described as best practices in the general UDI literature, many of which also apply specifically to students with ASD. Then, we will address a number of ideas that have been presented in scholarship focused on teaching college students with ASD.

Applicable UDI Strategies

Create a Positive Class Climate

There are several things you can do to set up a positive class environment for all students. Beginning with your syllabus, provide a carefully worded statement about accommodations. Your institution may have template language, or you could ask for advice from your office for students with disabilities. Take time in the first class to talk about the statement, making clear that working with students on accommodations is something that you are happy to do—not just a legal requirement you take on begrudgingly (Burgstahler 2017). Sadly, the latter approach is the case with some faculty, which frequently discourages students from seeking out the accommodations they need.

In addition to the accommodations statement, consider including a civility statement and discussing expectations for classroom behavior in class (Barnhill 2016; Gobbo and Shmulsky 2012; Sarrett 2017; Scott, McGuire, and Shaw 2003). This does two things. First, it reminds all students that they need to be respectful of everyone, regardless of differences, including not only those with disabilities but also those from different social and cultural backgrounds. Being clear on classroom behavior may be especially important for students with ASD who may not know the unwritten rules of how a college classroom works (especially where those rules differ from high school) and would benefit from an explicit statement of those expectations (Burgstahler and Russo-Gleicher 2015; Zager et al. 2013). Also, make sure you consistently enforce the expectations you have laid out. As we have discussed before, many individuals with ASD are strongly rule oriented and can become irritated when others fail to follow the rules, as shown by this example from one of the students from our own program.

STUDENT VOICES

In a classroom setting, one thing that would be beneficial is if the professors were more strict with talking rules. Listening to sidebar conversations and whispers is extremely distracting. It would be a nice positive change to be more strict with the policy.—**Anon**

Related UDI principle: Instructional climate

Use Both Verbal and Written Communication

Make sure you are using verbal and written communication for both content and instructions (Burgstahler 2017). Provide written instructions for all assignments as well as much written backup for lecture/discussion as possible (Shaw 2011). This could include posting slide presentations, your own lecture outlines or notes, or arranging for a note taker from among the students in the class (Parker 2012). A couple of good suggestions we have seen for finding students who are willing to serve as a note taker are to either offer extra credit or make it count toward class participation credit (Gravel et al. 2015; Scott, McGuire, and Shaw 2003). If possible, these should either be provided online before class (slides/lecture outline) or as soon as possible following class (notes). This is a general technique that benefits many students, but for those with ASD, it allows them to preview or review information to help them absorb it better.

Related UDI principle: Equitable use

Use a Variety of Instruction Methods

Utilizing various instruction methods is a general UDI principle that acknowledges that different people learn better in different ways (Burgstahler 2017; Scott, McGuire, and Shaw 2003). If you mix up how information is presented (lecture, video, readings, hands-on exercise, group work, etc.), each student in the class is likely to find a method that works well for their learning style some of the time. In the case of students with ASD, a fast-moving lecture may be hard to process (Zager et al. 2013), while methods that allow them to work at their own pace are often going to be better. An ASD-specific suggestion from Remy and Seaman (2014) is to include a "reflective activity, such as a worksheet, as an alternative to the social, interactive nature of active learning." In an article about applying UDL principles to library instruction, Ying Zhong (2012) described how she incorporated multiple modes into an instruction session about Boolean operators. She included a verbal description, diagrams, a quick physical activity, and time for trying a hands-on example. This demonstrates that although we have included this strategy under the section for courses rather than single sessions, it can be applied to both circumstances.

STUDENT VOICES

In the classroom, I learn better from examples. Showing experience videos (not lecture videos) and hands-on experiences are how I learn. It is extremely beneficial when the professor is interactive with the class. Movement is good!—**Emma Billingsley**

We do want to address group work here, because it is often mentioned as a good method in articles describing UDI (Gravel et al. 2015; Parker 2012). However, this is not a strong point for many with ASD, because of the social and communication challenges that we have discussed in prior chapters. We certainly do not suggest that you excuse autistic students from group work, as this is a reality of not only many college classes but also of many employment environments! If you have a student that you suspect has ASD, there are things that you can do to provide extra support. First of all, do not assume that *any* of your students know how to work well in teams. You may need to teach the entire class tips for group work—explicitly discussing issues like dividing tasks fairly and making decisions as a group (Gobbo and Shmulsky 2012). You can also choose to assign team members, looking for one or more people whom you believe can model good teamwork (especially someone with strong soft and/or organizational skills) to be in a group with a classmate with ASD (Wolf, Brown, and Bork 2009). You can also develop a list of specific roles to be divided among team members. If you think it is necessary, assign the team member with ASD a role that he or she is likely to be successful in (Wolf, Brown, and Bork 2009; Zager et al. 2013). For an example of a highly structured group project that included many supports for successful teamwork, see the chapter by Gravel et al. (2015) in the Recommended Reading section at the end of the chapter.

Related UDI principle: Flexibility in use

Provide Variety in Homework and Assignments

Providing variety in homework and graded assignments is another of the basic principles of UDI. It proposes that rather than relying on any one way of evaluating students, the professor mixes assignment types up a lot, giving each student an opportunity to learn to be assessed on some material in a way that suits his or her learning style. This is a tricky strategy to employ with students with ASD. On the one hand, it can benefit them by making sure that a course is not too dependent on assignments with which they might struggle—like presentations or group work. In this case, providing other types of assignments where they might show their strengths would be helpful. But on the other hand, many students with ASD thrive on consistency, so constantly changing up the types of homework and assignments may actually lead to anxiety. So, use this approach with caution! Nevertheless, here are some examples. For homework, in addition to readings, try watching videos, listening to podcasts, working through a tutorial, filling out worksheets, or completing hands-on search activities (Shaw 2011). Also be creative in offering a variety of graded work. In addition to papers, quizzes, and tests, consider things as varied as attendance at events, community or campus service, short informal writing assignments, presentations, or group projects (Burgstahler 2017; Highee 2015),

Related UDI principle: Flexibility in use

Take the Stress Out of Tests

Reducing test anxiety is another example of a UDI principle that could benefit many students. Not only is extra time on tests a common accommodation for students with a variety of disabilities, but many students find timed testing very stressful. We have found several excellent suggestions related to this. One is to allow unlimited time on tests for everyone (Izzo and Bauer 2015; Shaw 2011). This can be done either by having you or a proctor available until everyone is done (not possible in every testing situation) or by making the test a take-home. If a test does need to fit into a certain time period, try to design it so that it has time and a half or double time built in; for instance, create a test you think should take an hour for a 1.5- or 2-hour window (Scott, McGuire, and Shaw 2003; Shaw 2011). Jeanne Highee (2015) implemented this idea in a first-year experience course and reported that all the students who had an accommodation for extended test-taking time instead elected to take the tests with the rest of the class (and did as well as other students). Another suggestion is to allow students to create and bring one page of notes (Izzo and Bauer 2015). This may particularly help students with ASD, because creating the page can help them organize the material and their thoughts and may also reduce text anxiety.

Related UDI principle: Tolerance for error

ASD-Specific Strategies

THOUGHTS FROM OUR EXPERT: WORKING WITH STUDENTS WITH ASD

Cherie Fishbaugh, MA, BCBA, BS-L (PA)

Utilizing best practices during instruction is beneficial to all students. Providing visual supports and including active student responding is most helpful. When teaching, include the use of guided notes, graphic organizers, tangible learning, and explicit instruction. In addition, be sure to include resources, and be clear with instructions on how to access them. Students with ASD are very literal; thus encouragement of when and how to access resources is important. Example: You may call the writing center Monday–Friday from 8 a.m. to 3 p.m. to schedule an appointment or go online at any time to schedule. Same-day appointments are often available; however, during midterm and final weeks plan at least 72 hours in advance to ensure an appointment.

The More Structure the Better

The more organized the course is overall, the better it is for students with ASD (Gobbo and Shmulsky 2014). Start with a very clear and detailed syllabus that covers not only the format of the course but also classroom procedures (Burgstahler and Russo-Gleicher 2015). Provide a detailed schedule. If you need to make changes to the class schedule, do it as far ahead as possible (and in writing, not just verbally) (Gobbo and Shmulsky 2012; Zager et al. 2013). One suggestion we love is to go an extra step on the class calendar and use Google calendar or another online app, rather than just providing a typed schedule in the syllabus (Parker 2012). Not only does this allow you to make the calendar very visual by color coding items by category (readings, assignments, quizzes, etc.), but it is also much easier for students to be aware of changes. Students can simply use the link to see the updates, rather than logging into the CMS to download an updated schedule.

Structure can also be provided by making daily or weekly routines as regular as possible. Gobbo and Shmulsky (2014) suggest using both a daily routine (e.g., starting and ending class in the same manner) and/or a weekly routine (e.g., quizzes always fall on the same day of the week).

Another tip that we like related to structure is to choose textbooks carefully. Look for texts that provide features like outlines, study questions, and glossaries. Those features supply extra structure that will support many students, including those with ASD (Burgstahler 2017; Gravel et al. 2015). If available, an online textbook may allow students to employ assistive technology.

TIPS FROM OUR EXPERT: PROVIDE STRUCTURE FOR ASSIGNMENTS

Cherie Fishbaugh, MA, BCBA, BS-L (PA)

Assignments and projects can elicit anxiety for many students, especially those with ASD. Here are some tips to help decrease anxiety as well as promote a positive experience for both professor and student.

- Use your syllabus as a vehicle of communication. Note on your syllabus "subject to change," and identify objectives/subtopics per week/lecture. Identify due dates and have description of assignment.

- Provide a detailed rubric for each assignment.

- Use the rubric to provide corrective feedback to the student.

- Allow the student to explain their interpretation of the assignment directions.
- Provide immediate, direct feedback to the student.

Related UDI principle: Simple and intuitive instruction

Tap into Interests

We have already mentioned that one academic strength of many individuals with autism is a passionate interest in certain topics and a willingness to put a great deal of time into becoming an expert on those topics. Why not tap this strength if possible? Gobbo and Shmulsky (2014) suggest that faculty provide opportunities for students with ASD to pursue passions or show strengths in certain assignments. This could be implemented in two ways. The first is by allowing students a great deal of flexibility in selecting topics for research-based projects. The second way is by presenting multiple options for the format a project could be completed in. For example, a student with a strong background in technology could present a project as a web page or a video, or a student with a passion for art could produce something in a visual format.

Related UDI principle: Flexibility in use

"Attend to the Emotional Climate"

This suggestion is taken directly from an excellent article by Gobbo and Shmulsky (2014), which we have included in the Recommended Reading at the end of the chapter. The idea is that if the professor is aware of the factors that cause stress in a student with ASD, he or she can either try to mitigate those factors and/or keep an eye out for signs that a student with ASD is feeling stressed. Of course, this is only possible under certain circumstances. Not only do you first need to know that a student has ASD, but you would have had to have had a fairly in-depth conversation with the student to know what circumstances induce anxiety and how to assist the student in managing the stress.

Related UDI principle: Instructional climate

"Two Card Technique"

This approach comes from a book by Wolf, Brown, and Bork (2009), and was also a suggestion from our own local expert. It is a technique meant for working with students with ASD who are communicating too much in class. Maybe they ask too many questions, dominate the discussion, or tend to go off topic and speak too long. The idea is that you make two cards (perhaps laminated) that can be used throughout the semester. Each time the student asks or responds to a question they set aside a card. When the cards are all used, they know they need to hold other questions or comments until the end of class or your office hours. Of course, it does not have to always be two cards. In classes where discussion is regularly a major component, five cards might be more appropriate. A similar type of technique that has been suggested is hand signals (Zager et al. 2013). Tapping the wrist could be a subtle signal for a student who tends to provide responses that are too long. Another signal could be used for when the student has gone too far off topic. These techniques have the same limitations as "attend to the emotional climate"—they require prior knowledge and discussion with the student.

Related UDI principle: A community of learners

Addressing a Lack of Interaction

We just discussed class management strategies for when a student with ASD is interacting too much in class. Some students with ASD may go to the other extreme and not engage in class discussion at all. There are two main reasons this might occur. First, the student may not feel comfortable with participating in the discussion because classroom discussion is a complex social interaction with its own set of rules. Second, the speed at which questions are being asked or at which the discussion is moving may not be providing them with enough time to process the information and formulate responses. Here are a few strategies that may help:

- Provide some discussion questions in writing. This could be ahead of time in the course management system, on a piece of paper at the beginning of class, or even writing impromptu questions on the board. This gives all students in the class, not just those with ASD, some extra time to think about the questions and formulate answers (Zager et al. 2013).

- Participation does not always have to equal talking. Some credit could be given for answering questions that are provided in a print format either at the beginning or end of class. Or you could have the students participate by posing the questions (again in writing).

- Offer credit for participating in online postings and discussions (Robertson and Ne'eman 2008). As with providing questions in writing, this benefits those who need more time to process information. But, because it removes the face-to-face component, it also helps those who are not comfortable joining the class discussion—including those who are simply shy (Shaw 2011)!

Related UDI principle: A community of learners

Keep Expectations Equal

Keep in mind that your expectations and grading should be the same for students with ASD or any student with a disability (Remy and Seaman 2014). Wolf, Brown, and Bork (2009) point out that sometimes faculty members can subconsciously be unfair in grading (in either of two extremes). On the one hand, professors may give a student with ASD, or a physical or learning disability, a "break" when grading, by being less strict. This should not be the case, because while all students deserve the support and accommodations that help them succeed, they are still expected to meet the same standards as all other students in terms of attendance, assignments, projects, etc. At the opposite end of the spectrum, others may grade students who have certain accommodations harder (i.e., make an assumption that they should perform better than other students because they have accommodations like extra test-taking time). This is also unfair, because the accommodations are not advantages or cheats; they exist to level the playing field and put students in a position to be equal to their classmates.

Related UDI principle: Instructional climate

TEACHING ONLINE

Librarians teach online in a variety of ways: being the professor of record for completely online credit-bearing courses, being embedded in another professor's course, developing tutorials or other materials for specific classes, or simply creating online guides and videos that one hopes will be useful for both distance students and those who come to campus. As with teaching in-person, the amount of control the librarian has over the teaching environment and the amount of time he or she can dedicate to creating materials varies greatly. In some cases, a librarian may have great freedom to design an online guide or an entire course in the course management system. In other cases, they may inherit material developed by another librarian or professor or have to follow very strict guidelines for the look and feel of materials.

In many ways, online education is an excellent match for individuals with ASD. It supports their needs in all three areas where they tend to run into difficulties (social/communication, executive functioning/information processing, and environmental sensitivities). First, it eliminates the need for face-to-face communication with the professor and other students in the course and the social anxiety interaction might cause (Richardson 2017). Second, online courses are often very structured. The fact that all class materials need to be uploaded into a course management system naturally lends itself to a structured class. Having the entire course available from the beginning is helpful for those who need extra time to process information, allowing students with ASD to start early and move at their own pace (Catalano 2014). Finally, online content also allows a student with sensory difficulties to control his or her own environment. Rather than being stuck in a classroom where noises, lights, patterns, textures, or smells could provide a significant distraction, they can work wherever they want and adjust that environment to make it an optimal work space (Burgstahler and Russo-Gleicher 2015). Therefore, it is not surprising that in a study of learning preferences, students with ASD had a marked preference for online courses, in contrast to neurotypical students who had a preference for face-to-face interaction (Satterfield, Lepage, and Ladjahasan 2015). Another recent 2017 study showed that students with ASD did just as well as neurotypical students when taking online modules, both in terms of successful completion rates and grades earned (Richardson 2017). Having said all that, please do not take it as an indication that you will only encounter students with ASD in the online environment! Despite all the research cited above, many students with ASD really want to have that traditional on-campus college experience. The fast-growing popularity of our own campus programs and others across the country attest to that.

Our first tip related to teaching online is to simply encourage academic librarians to start, continue, or increase their production of online tools to support students. As we mentioned in Chapter 3, chat or email reference services may be a good option for students with ASD who hesitate to approach the reference desk. Online FAQs may also provide support in this way. All these options allow a student with a specific question to seek out an answer without having to figure out whom to approach and how to manage the social interaction. Online guides, tutorials, and videos also provide support for students who might want to learn materials at a slower pace and/ or in a controlled environment.

Some of the techniques we discussed above also apply well to online instruction. For those developing online guides or tutorials, these strategies include:

- Using direct, literal language when writing.
- Using multiple teaching methods (especially adding visual/graphic components).
- Covering only what is really needed.

The use of multiple teaching methods is well illustrated by a project completed by librarians at East Carolina University, who used UDL principles to construct a tutorial using LibGuides software (Webb and Hoover 2015). Throughout the pages of the tutorial, they worked to incorporate four different learning methods: text, visual (usually images, such as cartoons), audio, and kinesthetic (click-through tutorials). Their experience shows that librarians can construct UDI-based materials using software commonly found in libraries and without requiring sophisticated technological skills.

There are also a number of strategies that were addressed above for longer courses that would apply equally well to an entirely online course built in a course management system.

- Providing structure with a clear syllabus and calendar.
- Including a positive statement about accommodations.
- Using a variety of both teaching methods and assignments (both graded and ungraded).
- Providing extra structure for group work—yes, even if online!
- Allowing expanded or unlimited time on tests.

Beyond these strategies, the literature related to both UDI in online teaching and teaching students with ASD online focuses heavily on providing as much structure as possible. Specifically, providing a clear structure and organization for the course in the course management system is mentioned repeatedly, including the need to divide material into multiple pages, keep each page uncluttered, provide titles/headings for each page, and use consistent layout across pages (Burgstahler 2018; Catalano 2014; UDI Online Project 2009). In addition to the consistent structure, also consider creating an introduction (written, audio, or video) for both the course as a whole and each unit (Highee 2015). One suggestion that we thought might be especially useful for students with ASD was to set the course site to send regular reminders to the students of approaching assignment deadlines (UDI Online Project 2009).

A second area of emphasis in the literature that applies particularly well to students with ASD focuses on providing clear instructions and expectations in an online course (Burgstahler 2018). This does seem especially important in an online environment where students cannot seek out clarification in person during class or office hours. In regard to graded assignments, providing examples of good work, practice tests, and/or rubrics helps students know the expectations for the class. In particular, provide very clear instructions regarding posting to discussion boards or for online group work (Catalano 2014; UDI Online Project 2009). Finally, in an article specific to modifying an online research course to support students with special needs, Amy Catalano (2014) suggests providing a printable handout with detailed instructions (and graphics) for how to use library databases or any other new technologies (including potentially parts of the CMS itself!).

THOUGHTS FROM OUR EXPERT: ONLINE CONTENT

Cherie Fishbaugh, MA, BCBA, BS-L (PA)

It is important that resources be clear and concrete. When providing guides, use an outline format so it can serve as a checklist for the student. In addition, when setting up web pages, remember "less is best." This means that too many pictures, icons, and graphics can actually deter a student from the site. It causes an overstimulation, which overwhelms them, thus leading to frustration and avoidance of the site. Students benefit from visual aids; therefore, having handouts/guided notes of important tips/steps for the tutorials would be beneficial.

CONCLUSION

As with our chapter on providing research assistance, we think there are two major takeaways here for librarian instructors. The first is that students with ASD do have some specific learning needs, including some that are not commonly seen among the wider group of neurotypical students. The second is that meeting those needs does not have to mean completely reinventing how you teach. Although we have provided many different strategies for supporting students with ASD, we certainly do not expect that any librarian is going to employ all or perhaps even a majority of them! We encourage you to try implementing a few that suit both the type of instruction you provide and your own teaching style. No single teaching style suits every teacher, any more than it suits every student! But with a little bit of effort, you can find some strategies that will benefit not just students with ASD but also a wide range of students with various learning styles, leading to a better instruction experience for all.

RECOMMENDED READING

Gobbo, Ken, and Solvegi Shmulsky. 2014. "Faculty Experience with College Students with Autism Spectrum Disorders." *Focus on Autism and Other Developmental Disabilities* 29, no. 1: 13–22. https://doi.org/10.1177/1088357613504989.

This is a short article, but it packs in a lot of information about students with ASD and suggestions for working with them. It would be a great read for a librarian who teaches longer courses—or as a suggested read for a professor with a student with ASD in class.

Gravel, Jenna W., Laura A. Edwards, Christopher J. Buttimer, and David H. Rose. 2015. "Universal Design for Learning in Postsecondary Education: Reflections on Principles and Their Application." In *Universal Design in Higher Education: From Principles to Practice*, 2nd ed., ed. Sheryl E. Burgstahler. Cambridge, MA: Harvard Education Press.

This chapter is essentially a case study of how a group of professors changed a traditional lecture course to adopt many UDI practices. There are many excellent ideas in here, but we especially like the detailed description of how they fostered teamwork skills in a group project.

Scott, Sally S., Joan M. McGuire, and Stan F. Shaw. 2003. "Universal Design for Instruction—A New Paradigm for Adult Instruction in Postsecondary Education." *Remedial and Special Education* 24, no. 6: 369–379. https://doi.org/10.1177/07419325030240060801.

This is one of several articles published by the team at the University of Connecticut who developed Universal Design for Instruction. It is our favorite because it does a great job of explaining why changing student demographics are impacting university education and providing a history of UD.

FIVE

Student Employees with ASD in the Library

Numerous studies have investigated various aspects of people with ASD and employment, including job outlook, strengths and weaknesses as employees, the law and employment supports, and best management styles. It is especially important to remember that in the context of employment much of this research addresses adults who span the spectrum, including those who have severe symptoms and intellectual disabilities. Although a few studies have focused on those with Asperger's (pre-2013 designation) or who are "high-functioning," we have had to draw from the broader body of research in order to form a more complete picture. Therefore, please keep in mind that the potential employees we are discussing are college students. Each student had to have the academic credentials to be accepted into college. Although they will likely show at least some common characteristics of autism, they are also quite likely to be of average or above average intelligence. In other words, the students with ASD on your campus will represent the same "spectrum" of intelligence and abilities as the full student body. Reading a full list of potential problems that a student with ASD *might* have can be daunting, so it is important to remember that most students may exhibit only a few of those characteristics and that by the time they have reached college, many of them have had years of support from professionals to help them manage those symptoms. By the end of this chapter we hope that readers will see students with ASD as potentially the best student employees they may ever have.

JOB OUTLOOK FOR INDIVIDUALS WITH ASD

The employment outlook for adults with ASD is terrible. Roux et al. (2013) report that just 53.4 percent of young adults with autism had held paid work outside of the home in the eight years following high school. A similar study (Shattuck et al.) in 2012 reinforced these findings, with only 55.1 percent of participants having found paid employment in the six years after high school. Both studies also conclude that young adults on the autism spectrum have a lower rate of employment *even compared to young adults with other disabilities*. Equally disturbing are the outcomes specific to college graduates. In an Australian study, 45 percent of college-graduate participants were found to be employed in positions for which they were overqualified (Baldwin, Costley, and Warren 2014). Not only do individuals with ASD have unusual difficulty in finding jobs, but they often end up working in positions that do not meet their educational levels.

One potential bright spot in this picture was provided by a study (Taylor and Seltzer 2010) on the employment status of recent high school graduates. Of the young adults that were pursuing a college degree, 78 percent were also holding a competitive part-time job. This seems to suggest that a majority of college students with ASD are not only capable of securing and maintaining employment but are also balancing it with their coursework. The ability of college students with ASD to gain and maintain employment is also confirmed by the experience of students in our own university's support program—16 of the 21 program participants had either an internship or paid employment for the summer of 2018. As we will discuss in this chapter, the majority of issues that workers with ASD face are social in nature. This leads us to believe that college work experience is probably even more essential to students with ASD than most. Employment during college can help these students tremendously by exposing them to the unwritten norms of a work environment and introducing them to many types of common work-related social interactions with supervisors, fellow employees, and the public. If your library gives a student with ASD an opportunity via a job, you may not only end up with a fantastic employee, but you may also potentially have a very positive impact on that student's future success as an employee.

STUDENTS WITH ASD AS EMPLOYEES

The following sections contain an overview of characteristics, both strengths and weaknesses, which might be seen in student employees with

ASD. Once again, please remember that actual student employees will most likely only show some of these traits and the level of intensity of each trait will vary. This variability was reflected in a case study of two adults with ASD who were employed in an academic library (Miner 2009). It described two employees who had worked in different departments in the library. The differences between the two employees were striking. One was described as needing a quiet space to work, preferring to interact with only one person at a time, and enjoying tasks of a repetitive nature over a long period. The second employee was outgoing and enjoyed working with the public and liked having a variety of tasks to complete during the day. The lesson here is to always remember that people with autism are individuals. Just like neurotypical employees, each person comes with his or her own personality, abilities, quirks, talents, and areas for improvement.

Potential Challenges

The most common difficulties experienced by employees with autism fall into three broad categories: social interactions, executive functioning, and environmental sensitivity. As we discussed in Chapter 1, problems with social interactions and understanding social cues are a hallmark of ASD. This can manifest in many different ways that may affect their interactions with either the public or fellow employees. Here are some potential examples:

- Inability to make eye contact while talking to someone
- Standing too close/being in someone's personal space
- Trouble reading others' facial expression, body language, or tone of voice (e.g., someone shifting away to signal discomfort or a desire to end an interaction)
- Maintaining proper levels of grooming/hygiene (e.g., disheveled appearance or body odor)
- Either too brusque or too talkative, thus potentially appearing either rude in the first case or inappropriately friendly in the second
- Problems understanding idioms and certain types of humor (e.g., sarcasm or irony)
- Changing the topic into an area of personal interest that is not related to the situation at hand
- Repetitive behaviors, which are more likely to appear in new or stressful situations

These types of behaviors may be problematic, especially in jobs where employees deal with the public frequently. In an academic library context, this would include anyone who works at a circulation desk, other service point, or administrative offices. As anyone who works in an academic library knows, the circulation desk or other public service desk is often the first point of contact for students. In many academic libraries these service points are primarily staffed by students during a great part of the day and night. Although a supervisor is usually nearby, they are not always immediately present and able to assist. Therefore, our student workers are an integral part of our libraries' public image and customer service, especially with other students. Sometimes students hesitate to approach an adult who is clearly older than they are and may specifically look for a student employee, because they feel more comfortable asking a question of someone their own age. If a patron's initial interaction at a service desk is poor, they may be hesitant to seek out assistance in the future. Supervisors have a legitimate reason to be concerned about how all student employees interact with patrons and need to be aware that employees with ASD may exhibit behaviors that they have not encountered in student employees before. Supervisors should also keep in mind that interactions with other employees can also be problematic for workers with ASD. In fact, in many cases, difficulties dealing with coworkers or supervisors were cited as the primary job performance issues for employees with ASD and sometimes even lead to the termination of the worker (Hendricks 2010; Kirchner and Dziobek 2014; Müller et al. 2003).

The second category where employees with ASD may have difficulties in work situations is executive functioning (Hendricks 2010). We discussed executive functioning in more detail in Chapters 1 and 3. To review, executive functioning is an umbrella term that encompasses a number of neurological skills relating to self-regulation and control. Executive functioning can also have an impact on a number of skills related to work:

- **Adjusting to Changes in the Work Environment or New Routines** (Hendricks 2010; Hendrickx 2010; Müller et al. 2003): Student workers with ASD may take longer to adjust to a new work environment. In addition to the need to learn new schedules and routines, they also need to adjust to a new physical environment (see more below) and social environment, both of which they may find more stressful than most neurotypical employees.

- **Learning Multistep Processes:** This is related to not only executive functioning but also information processing issues we discussed in Chapters 3 and 4. Individuals with ASD may need a bit of extra time to process information, especially if instructions are provided only verbally. There is a great deal of library work that involves multistep processes, so it is a potential issue to keep in mind.

- **Time Management and Setting Priorities When Assigned Multiple Tasks** (Hendrickx 2010; Howlin, Alcock, and Burkin 2005): If your student worker has certain tasks that they need to complete during a given shift or week, they may need some extra help with prioritizing which tasks to address first or how much time to spend on each one.

- **Transitioning to New Tasks** (Baldwin, Costley, and Warren 2014; Howlin, Alcock, and Burkin 2005; Miner 2009): The ability to do these things taps into the same set of executive functioning skills as time management/setting priorities. Some student workers with ASD may need more explicit instructions on what to do when a particular task is finished. They may also struggle when working in situations where they are likely to be interrupted by patrons, as at the circulation desk or other service point. This forces them to constantly reset their focus.

The third category where employees with ASD may face difficulties at work is with environmental and sensory issues. This is due to hyperreactivity to sensory input (DSM-5 2013; Hendricks 2010). Although we discussed these issues in great detail in Chapter 2, it is worth mentioning one particular survey in which workers with ASD were asked to identify factors that interfered with their work performance. A majority reported having sensory issues at work, including problems with noise (64 percent), lighting (51 percent), and smell (60 percent). Fifty-nine percent also mentioned shared working space as a negative factor (Kirchner and Dziobek 2014). For neurotypical individuals these types of factors may present small annoyances, but for those with ASD they may be a major obstacle to working productively.

Strengths as Employees

At this point, if you are a supervisor, you may be feeling hesitant about hiring a student with ASD; however, these individuals also come with strengths that balance many of the weaknesses and make them valuable employees. In fact, a very interesting 2017 article in *The Chronicle of Higher Education* reported that a number of large companies had begun programs actively seeking employees with ASD, believing that the skills and dispositions they brought (including honesty, attention to detail, and focus) more than made up for any required workplace modifications (Basken 2017).

When it comes to the evidence for the strengths of individuals with ASD as employees, much of it is anecdotal or based on smaller studies. This may partially be due to the fact that individuals with autism are just that—individuals, with a wide range of interests and strengths that suit a variety of job types. However, a great deal of blame may also be attributed to the tendency of scholarship on ASD to focus on diagnosis and treatment. This naturally leads to research that centered on the diagnostic criteria of ASD, which focus on the negative, rather than looking for strengths or advantages that may also be common characteristics. Indeed, although we were able to find numerous studies regarding employment, only one of those studies directly studied the particular work-related aptitudes of those with ASD. Nevertheless, we have found evidence for some intriguing positive characteristics.

Although students with ASD may struggle with social interactions, this may also mean that they are also less likely to engage in common social distractions (e.g., chatting with fellow students instead of working) or problematic social behavior. For instance, in various studies, employees with ASD have received praise for being honest and not engaging in "office-politics" (Baldwin, Costley, and Warren 2014; Hillier, Campbell, and Mastriani 2007; Howlin, Alcock, and Burkin 2005). Another study highlighted not only authenticity (honesty) as a signature strength for those with autism but also open-mindedness (thinking things through rather than jumping to conclusions) and fairness (specifically treating all people the same) (Kirchner, Ruch, and Dziobek 2016). All of these are very positive traits for communicating not only with coworkers but with a diverse group of patrons.

Additionally, employees with ASD are consistently cited for having an excellent work ethic. Not only are they credited with low levels of absenteeism and high punctuality but also for dependability, reliability, consistency, and for being conscientious (Baldwin, Costley, and Warren 2014; Hillier, Campbell, and Mastriani 2007). So far, we are developing a picture of employees who can be counted on to actually show up for work when scheduled, focus on that work once they are there, plus be honest and open minded.

So, employees with ASD tend to be reliable, which is good, but not necessarily an extraordinary characteristic among student workers. But we are not done yet. There are other strengths that are particularly applicable to library work. Research has indicated that individuals with autism also tend to have strong technical and logical reasoning skills, as well as excelling at detail-oriented work, including tasks that involve visual acuity (sharpness of vision) (Hagner and Cooney 2005; Howlin, Alcock, and Burkin 2005; Lorenz and Heinitz 2014; Müller et al. 2003). In addition to that, some are also attributed with a higher threshold than usual for tackling and even enjoying repetitive work (Hagner and Cooney 2005; Parr and Hunter 2014; Robertson and Ne'eman 2008). So . . . detail-oriented, repetitive work, including tasks requiring visual acuity—I believe that we have just described a majority of work done in academic libraries and about 90 percent of the work that is specifically done by student workers.

Those last strengths really stick out, don't they? In fact, several articles have suggested library work as an excellent match for individuals on the spectrum. Baldwin, Costley, and Warren (2014) specifically suggest librarian (along with architect and computer programmer) as an occupation that may suit adults with ASD, because it is a job that requires "visual thinking, systematic information processing or precise technical abilities." Another study of the special interests of individuals with ASD also supports that they often prefer a "systemizing approach" (any approach relating to working with a system or systems) (Kirchner, Ruch, and Dziobek 2016). This was certainly the case with a student intern with ASD who worked at our own music library. The staff person who supervised the student commented on how well he did on the call number system training program used to train all student workers, scoring one of the best scores he had seen. Not only that, but the same student, based on that training, actually noticed a book that had been mislabeled with an incorrect call number and brought it to the supervisor's attention, greatly impressing the supervisor.

Once again, considering how much library work is based on systems, such as subject headings, call numbers, and database searching, not to even mention all the spreadsheets we produce, one can start to see that many aspects of academic library work might be appealing to individuals with ASD. A study we found that focuses on autistic workers' self-reported strengths supports this. The authors of the article surveyed and compared individuals with autism (technically Asperger's due to the date of the study) to a neurotypical group (Lorenz and Heinitz 2014). They found that 73 of 136 respondents with ASD (54 percent) characterized attention to detail as a strength. In comparison, only 34 of 155, or 22 percent, of the neurotypical respondents reported the same. Think of the amount of work (again, often completed by students) in an academic library that requires this skill, including book preparation, shelving, shelf reading, digitizing, and gathering statistics. Such employees would be extremely valuable in many academic library departments—circulation, cataloging, serials, systems, electronic resources, and even special collections. In the same survey, the other most highly cited strengths would also contribute positively to many types of library work—logical reasoning, focus, systemizing, consistency, and visual skills. Obviously, an individual who has natural abilities that allow them to excel at detailed and systematized work and enjoys doing it for extended periods of time would be an extremely valuable employee.

Two case studies that we were able to locate of adults with ASD working in an academic library highlight this. The first, also mentioned above, reported on two employees who worked in different departments. Both received positive reviews, and in one case the library extended the fixed work period by several months (Miner 2009). The authors of the second article were thrilled with their employee who had been hired to work in the stacks, saying he performed "an excellent job of the work that 10 students had previously not been doing well" (Strub and Stewart 2010). In particular, he excelled at shelf reading and shifting. In both cases, the employees receiving these great reviews were *not* college students and needed more support than would be expected for a college student with ASD. Therefore, it seems fair to expect that student workers on the spectrum could be equally or even more successful at academic library work.

Given the unique combination of strengths and weaknesses described above, there is likely going to be a natural tendency on the part of those who supervise student workers to pigeonhole potential workers with ASD into certain types of jobs—namely away from positions at service desks that work with the public and toward those in departments that work behind the scenes. Although the research supports that this is the very sort of work that may sometimes suit these students the best, we nevertheless want to argue passionately *against* doing this, or more specifically, against assigning employees with ASD *only* tasks that do not force them to interact with other workers or the public. First, not every individual with ASD wants to be in a job where they spend most of their time working by themselves. Some may greatly enjoy the social contact of a job that involves working with the public. Take, for instance, Emma, who is a student in our university's own autism support program. She has already held a variety of jobs, all of which involve dealing with people:

STUDENT VOICES

Finding a job has been ok. I haven't struggle[d] that much and now that I have more experience it is becoming easier to find a job. I have worked at the swim club during the summers; this semester I was a phone-a-thon representative for my University's Foundation. I am looking forward to being a desk assistant next semester in my resident hall on campus.

—**Emma Billingsley**

Second, even if a particular student employee with ASD happens to excel at these types of tasks and feels more comfortable in a job that involves no patron contact, it might not necessarily be the best thing for that student. We need to remember the terrible employment statistics that we opened this chapter with—only slightly above 50 percent of young adults are employed in the years following high school (a worse outcome even compared to groups with other types of disabilities). Plus, those who do find employment are often underemployed; in one study of adults who were employed 70 percent reported "mental underload" (Kirchner, Ruch, and Dziobek 2016). In other words, more than two-thirds were not feeling sufficiently stimulated or challenged by the work they were doing. The hypothetical student workers we are discussing in this chapter are college students. Each and every one hopes to graduate and have a successful career and live independently, just like any other college student. Although some might be attracted to careers that have minimal contact with the public/customers, they will still need to be able to operate in a work environment and develop relationships with coworkers. College students with ASD *need* to be exposed to a real-world work environment that stretches their social skills and develops other necessary skills that will help them be successful in employment after college. In many cases, whether or not they gain or maintain employment will come down to their ability to handle social situations (Nasamran, Witmer, and Los 2017). Hiring students with ASD provides them the opportunity to improve their skills in working with the public. This is an invaluable experience for them that may have a great impact on their future employment status.

THOUGHTS FROM OUR EXPERT: EMPLOYEES WITH ASD

Cherie Fishbaugh, MA, BCBA, BS-L (PA)

Employers around the world are beginning to recognize the unique skills of individuals with autism and the benefits for their businesses. At the Autism at Work Summit in 2018, businesses such as Microsoft, Ford, Ernst and Young (EY), JP Chase and Morgan, DXC Technology, and SAP discussed these benefits, which included reduced staff turnover and increased productivity. Hiren Shukla, leader of EY's Neurodiversity Center of Excellence, stated that he found employing individuals on the spectrum increased morale and job satisfaction for other employees as well as made for better managers.

Rising Tide Car Wash in Florida employs over 80 individuals on the spectrum. The car wash has five times lower turnover and 20 percent higher loading efficiency than other car washes. It ranks 97th percentile in employee pride and 94th percentile in feedback culture. They took a car wash that served 35,000 cars a year to serving 150,000; to top that they opened another location that is on track to wash 200,000 this year (note they are less than 4 miles apart). Lastly, Rising Tide has had zero work-related injuries, as Tom D'Eri (cofounder and COO) states "because they follow the manual."

There are so many advantages to hiring individuals with autism. Their exceptional skills including attention to detail, ability to do routine tasks for long periods of time, perseverance, and extreme honesty and loyalty are only a few. People with autism see the world differently. Take the time to listen to their interpretations and problem-solving strategies—their analogies and metaphors that make sense after a comprehensive explanation. It's truly fascinating.

SUPPORTING STUDENT WORKERS WITH ASD

First, all employers need to remember that individuals with autism, just as others with disabilities, are protected from discrimination in hiring and employment by the Americans with Disabilities Act (ADA). Employers are required to provide employees with reasonable supports as long as it does not pose an undue burden. For more information on the ADA and individuals with ASD in the workplace, we strongly recommend the article by Wendy F. Hensel listed in this chapter's Recommended Reading section. Of course, not only is offering supports the law, but it is also simply the right thing to do. Very often a few simple measures are all that are needed to help an individual with disabilities be an excellent employee.

A support is a proactive and preventative measure that helps keep problems from arising in the first place (Hendrickx 2010). We already discussed one type of supports, academic accommodations, in Chapter 4 on library instruction. We will also return to the idea of supports for college students with ASD more broadly in Chapter 6 on outreach. Supports also play an important role for employees with ASD. The good news for employers is that there are many concrete strategies that managers can use to support student workers with ASD. You will find that many of them are not onerous or time consuming; it is more just a matter of knowing what issues may come up and addressing them directly and clearly. You may even find that some of the suggestions below are things that you have previously done with neurotypical workers. Also keep in mind that you do not need to reinvent the wheel! Many of these students may have been diagnosed with ASD while fairly young and may have had professional support developing strategies to be successful in a variety of situations, including employment. If a problem arises, the first step should always be to ask the student if he or she has had a similar problem in the past and what strategies were suggested for addressing it. Also, if the student is still working with a professional, especially someone who also works at your institution, ask for permission to initiate contact with that person. Not only might they have strategies to give you, but they may be able to help address the problem by working with the student directly.

STRATEGIES FOR SUPERVISORS

Start Out Strong

If possible, talk to the employee at the beginning of employment. If the student has disclosed that they have ASD, you can treat it as a formal "job description analysis" where you review the job responsibilities and discuss areas where the student thinks he or she may have difficulties (Hendrickx 2010). It would also be beneficial to specifically ask if they have any particular stressors, what their reaction to those stressors are, and ways to manage them (Organization for Autism Research 2012). This can provide you an opportunity to be very specific about what are acceptable and nonacceptable ways to handle things and have some support mechanisms in place from the beginning. If the student has not disclosed, but you suspect, you could still have a general discussion about job responsibilities and workplace behavior, but sticking to the same information that you would share with any new student employee. If you frequently work with student employees, this is probably something that you already do for everyone. If you are considering bringing up the topic of ASD with an individual who has not disclosed, we suggest you consult the advice presented by Sarah Hendrickx (2010) (see Recommended Reading at the end of this chapter).

We strongly recommend looking for a way to provide some basic autism awareness training to other employees (both student and regular staff) in your library (Müller et al. 2003). Frankly, we suggest that you do so even if you do not currently have any employees on the spectrum. If you are lucky, you may have a professional on campus that you can reach out to. For example, if you have an autism support program on campus, someone from that program might be able to provide a short training session for library employees. If not, you could check with your office of disability services to see if they have a professional on staff who works with students on the spectrum. If your college offers education degrees, a faculty member who specializes in special education might be an option. In certain cases, the new employee may even feel comfortable talking to coworkers and/or providing materials about ASD, though if he or she seems hesitant, please do not pressure them to share. Keep in mind that a student may feel comfortable talking about his or her own personal experience with autism but not comfortable serving as a spokesperson for ASD more broadly. If you cannot find anyone to offer training, you can always provide all employees with a short article or handout, along with an invitation to approach you with any questions. Your coworkers do not need to become experts on everything about ASD—they just need some basic awareness so they understand where the student is coming from and have some idea on how to support him or her. We have provided a sample handout (Appendix A) and have suggested an appropriate article in the Recommended Reading section.

Another idea is to consider assigning a coworker to be a mentor (Müller et al. 2003; Organization for Autism Research 2012). This provides the employee with a trusted person whom they can ask questions other than the direct supervisor. Not only might this be more comfortable for the student worker but can also potentially reduce the time burden of the supervisor (Wolf, Brown, and Bork 2009). This mentor could be either another student employee or a regular staff member, as long as they are generally available during the student's work hours. If your campus or library offers any sort of information program about ASD, the very best choice would be someone who had attended such a session. Additionally, the ideal mentor would be someone who himself or herself possesses strong "soft skills" and is adept at social interactions. Since individuals with ASD often struggle with unwritten social rules, this provides a safe person to introduce them to the norms of your library and guide them through potentially problematic situations.

Communication Tips

We have addressed communicating with students with ASD in both our research help and instruction chapters (Chapters 3 and 4), but the general principles bear repeating here. When communicating with students employees with ASD, you should always be direct. Do not assume that they will pick up meaning from your facial expression, body language, or tone of voice. Avoid using figurative speech and idioms. Keep in mind that individuals with ASD may have difficulty understanding when you are being ironic, sarcastic, or joking and may therefore incorrectly interpret what you are saying. Do not suggest or hint at things, but say them clearly and concisely (Hendrickx 2010; Müller et al. 2003).

This is also true if you need to point out mistakes or correct inappropriate behavior. Use the "kind, but direct" approach that we introduced in Chapter 3. Remain kind and calm in your tone of voice, but be straight to the point in your wording. If they are doing something that violates a social rule or norm, instead of just punishing them for the infraction, take the time to explain exactly what they did that was wrong and why it was wrong. Keep in mind that often an individual with ASD may be unaware that they were doing something inappropriate and did not mean to offend or break rules (Hensel 2017). Suggest or brainstorm alternative ways to handle similar situations in the future (Organization for Autism Research 2012). If applicable to the given situation, allow them to practice the alternative behavior with you.

Our own campus expert has reassured us again and again that while you may feel that you are being too blunt when speaking so frankly, perhaps even bordering on rudeness, individuals with ASD not only need you to be that clear but actually *appreciate* it. It is less confusing to them to have things spelled out rather than guess at someone's meaning. This is corroborated by a study on vocational supports by Müller et al. (2003), which reported:

> A number of participants reported frustration at the fact that supervisors—perhaps out of a desire to be polite—often expressed themselves indirectly and expected participants to second-guess their real meanings. Guessing the intentions of others is extremely difficult for individuals with ASDs, and the majority of participants stressed their preference for direct, even blunt, communication.

SAMPLE SCENARIO

The Problem: One student worker complains to you that another student worker (with ASD) is making him uncomfortable by constantly standing right next to him.

What Is Behind the Problem: If you are neurotypical, you probably have an innate sense of what is appropriate in terms of personal space and contact. You can make decisions on how close you stand next to someone and how you should touch them during communication (no contact versus handshake versus clap on the back versus hug), based on your relative statuses and relationship (family, close friend, acquaintance, coworker, supervisor). You probably do this subconsciously, without really having to think about it. For those who are neurotypical, these are the sort of social norms that we absorbed naturally when children. Individuals with ASD, however, often struggle with exactly this sort of thing. They need to have the rules (and the reasons behind them) verbally expressed so that they can make a conscious attempt to follow them.

Solution: As a supervisor in this situation, there are several things to keep in mind. First, understand that the student with ASD is not trying to intimidate the other student or make him feel uncomfortable. In fact, he probably has no idea that his actions could have this result. So you need to explain to the student three things: (1) the problem, (2) why it is a problem and what social norms are involved, and (3) provide an alternative behavior or a rule they can follow to guide them.

Sample Script:

1. You are making some of the other workers uncomfortable by standing too close.

2. Although people often feel comfortable sitting or standing right next to people they know really well (like family or close friends), in work settings they prefer to have more space between themselves and people they don't know well.

3. Since we are at work here, the latter rule applies. Please try to stand about 2 feet away. That is about an arm length away, or enough room that another person could walk between you without touching.

Reinforce: This is an example where you can reinforce the change by practicing with the student. First you could illustrate by walking up to the student and standing an appropriate distance away. Then let them try it a few times until they are comfortable with it.

The same approach should be taken if the student is behaving in an unusual way (e.g., employing a stim). It is better to simply ask why! It is unlikely to offend if the question is asked in a kind and nonjudgmental way, and it may help prevent a misunderstanding or issue down the road (Hendrickx 2010).

There is, of course, a line between providing appropriate supports for an individual and allowing behavior you would not accept in a neurotypical employee. Having ASD is not an excuse for repeated inappropriate behavior at work. Although the ADA, as mentioned earlier in this chapter, protects those with disabilities from discrimination and requires that employers provide supports, it does not cover misconduct, including "disruptive or threatening behavior" (Hensel 2017). Although an employee with ASD should be given leeway and support to help them adjust to the new social environment of the workplace, ultimately they should be expected to meet the same conduct standards and work expectations as all student workers, just as they will be expected to meet the standards of any workplace once they graduate (Hagner and Cooney 2005).

A related communication tip is to take time to explain things in more detail than you normally might. This is especially important when discussing aspects of the job related to social interactions. Be very specific on expected behaviors in a variety of situations. If possible, provide scripts rather than vague instructions (Hagner and Cooney 2005; Organization for Autism Research 2012). Do not assume that a student with ASD knows what it means to "be professional when answering the phone." Tell them exactly what they should say when they answer, when they put someone on hold, when they transfer the call, etc. Other examples of topics that should be addressed are how to communicate with various people (supervisor, coworker, patron), expectations for dress and hygiene (especially if your library does not have any sort of formal dress code), office routines, and rules for computer and phone use (Wolf, Brown, and Bork, 2009).

In some situations, especially patron interactions, it may also be useful to model behavior for them (Müller et al. 2003; Organization for Autism Research 2012). This is also a strategy we discussed earlier relating to providing research assistance and is strongly endorsed by our own campus expert. For instance, let the student spend some time observing you or an experienced coworker answer the phone or greet patrons at the desk; then ask the student worker to do so while you are present, following the script and examples. If they make mistakes, correct and have them try again until they are comfortable doing it on their own. The modeling strategy may be useful for other tasks as well, especially those containing multiple steps (Müller et al. 2003).

TIPS FROM OUR EXPERT

Cherie Fishbaugh, MA, BCBA, BS-L (PA)

It is important that the employee with ASD understand their job and what is expected of them. The following ideas can promote a successful working environment for a person on the spectrum:

- Consistency: including descriptions, jobs, and procedures (including what to do after the completion of the task(s).
- Concrete instructions: have detailed instructions for jobs/projects. If a job is variable, note the variables and options to approach.
- Explicit teaching of tasking when able (model, do together, and then have them do it independently).
- Set expectations for job, interactions, arrival, departure, etc.
- Provide clear deadlines to assist with time management.
- Use visual aids: including checklist, resource guides, organizational charts, etc.
- Understand and be considerate of sensory needs.
- If there is a change in the schedule or their responsibility, provide time for the employee to process, understand, and accept the change.
- Break complex, multistep tasks down into smaller steps.
- Set aside a specified time per day/week for employee to check in and assure them they can ask questions at any time.
- Provide immediate corrective feedback.

Tips Related to Time, Organization, and Space

When providing either a script or instructions on how to do a task, consider presenting documentation (Miner 2009; Organization for Autism Research 2012; Strub and Stewart 2010). Many individuals with ASD learn better visually than auditorily. Plus, as we have mentioned in Chapter 3, both poor handwriting (fine motor skills) and difficulties multitasking can make it difficult for some to take notes themselves. For tasks with multiple steps, a step-by-step list of instructions may be useful. If possible and appropriate, consider adding graphics to the text, like screenshots or photos. We acknowledge that this may prove time consuming, especially for short-term projects (Miner 2009), but keep in mind that such materials could also be useful in the future as training aids for new workers, including neurotypical employees. For other tasks, a checklist or even color-coded labels may serve to provide an extra bit of structure (Hagner and Cooney 2005; Hendricks 2010; Hendrickx 2010). We mentioned modeling behavior above. Similarly, if the employee will be producing written work, such as reports or spreadsheets, give them a model to work from. If creating detailed instructions or examples is too time consuming, an alternative would be to allow the student worker to use a digital recorder to record your verbal instructions, so that they can review them later (Hendrickx 2010).

An adherence to routine is one of the diagnostic criteria for ASD (DSM-5 2013). Therefore, employees with ASD may benefit from extra structure on the job (Müller et al. 2003; Wolf, Brown, and Bork 2009). If possible, a consistent schedule is a good idea. This could mean working set hours each day or week, rather than having hours vary from week to week. It may also mean allowing the student worker to approach his or her work in a consistent order, with a list of tasks they regularly follow (Hagner and Cooney 2005; Hendricks 2010; Strub and Stewart 2010). It should also be made clear what the employee should do once they finish work. Hagner and Cooney (2005) specifically suggest there be a "downtime alternative" in place—a specific task they routinely turn to if they complete all their scheduled assignments. Additionally, a regularly scheduled meeting time with the supervisor (and/or the mentor) can be beneficial (Hendrickx 2010; Müller et al. 2003). The meeting provides a time to discuss any issues or concerns either on the part of the supervisor or the student as well as an opportunity to provide praise for any tasks done well. Just as it is important to be direct and clear in instructions or criticism, praise also should be delivered explicitly (Organization for Autism Research 2012)! They are unlikely to intuit from your tone and body language that you are happy with their work, but need to hear it.

If the student worker has environmental sensitivities, there are often inexpensive and practical solutions that can help mitigate them. Noise and foot traffic near the work area can both be serious distractions. In ideal circumstances, a separate office with a door would be best; however, many academic libraries cannot provide this setup even for all full-time employee, much less student workers! Instead, look for a spot that is away from where people frequently pass through or congregate to chat (Miner 2009). If all else fails, consider a work area that faces the wall and headphones to help cancel the sound (Hendrickx 2010; Miner 2009). Sensitivity to smells could be combated with air-neutralizing sprays or a small air purifier. If bright fluorescent lights are proving problematic, a desk lamp or sitting near a window can help (Miner 2009). Computer screen glare can be reduced by a simple screen filter (Hendrickx 2010).

Overall, we feel that most of the supports listed above are simple and easily implemented. In fact, some may be things that you have already used or would be useful with neurotypical student employees as well. Communication is more a matter of awareness, making sure to be direct and taking a bit of time to provide extra details. Most of the suggestions for space and sensory supports are also straightforward and low cost. Supports related to executive functioning issues (time management and organization) may prove a bit more time intensive initially, but not every student worker on the spectrum is going to need this type of accommodation. In fact, in one study that involved interviewing the supervisors of employees with ASD, the managers not only gave employees with ASD very good reviews but also *did not find supervising them to be more problematic than supervising neurotypical employees* (Hagner and Cooney 2005). The authors of that study conclude that experienced supervisors are already used to supervising employees with a wide range of needs and differences and therefore are quite able to adapt to workers with ASD. Therefore, we feel that if you are reading this either as an experienced supervisor or even as someone who is willing to learn a bit about ASD (and since you have read this chapter, you must be!), you will not find managing a student worker on the spectrum any more challenging than managing your average neurotypical student worker.

CONCLUSION

We cannot, of course, guarantee that every student worker with ASD will be an excellent employee, any more than we could guarantee that with neurotypical student workers. They are still young adults, who vary greatly in levels of maturity and responsibility. Plus, each is an individual with his or her own strengths and weaknesses that will impact their work. However, as we discussed throughout this book so far, just as ASD tends to lead to certain common weaknesses, it also tends to lead to certain common strengths. The strength profile that emerges for employees is one of honesty, fairness, attention to detail, enjoying working within systems, ability to endure (or even appreciate) repetitive tasks, and reliability. That profile is certainly one that makes us believe that many students with ASD would make fine student employees in an academic library, with their strong points more than making up for a small amount of time spent on the supports that will help them be successful.

RECOMMENDED READING

Hendrickx, Sarah. 2010. *The Adolescent and Adult Neuro-Diversity Handbook: Asperger Syndrome, ADHD, Dyslexia, Dyspraxia, and Related Conditions*. Philadelphia: Jessica Kingsley.

> See Chapter 12 on the working environment. It has a good summary of common issues, a long list of ideas for supports, and a small section (pp. 172–173) that addresses how to handle a situation where an employee has not disclosed, but you suspect they are neurodiverse.

Organization for Autism Research. 2012. "Understanding Autism: An Employer's Guide." Accessed June 10. https://researchautism.org /resources/understanding-autism-an-employers-guide.

> This very short guide is perfect for providing some basic strategies to a supervisor or mentor.

SIX

Outreach, Support, and Staff Training: Working across Campus to Support Students with ASD

The academic library of today is a dynamic and interactive campus space and one whose staff spends an increasing amount of time reaching out to campus programs and offices. Library instruction and research is occurring not just within the library building but all over campus—in the embedded and flipped classrooms, in student success offices and programs, in distance education programs, and more. The library has always been a physical and virtual space that connects people, organizations, departments, and scholarly conversations. Collaborating with many different groups on campus promotes the library's services as well as positive relationships between the library and students, faculty, and campus offices. Outreach is becoming more specialized and more widespread. Therefore, for academic libraries, students with autism represent another opportunity to expand the reach of their services.

According to the American Library Association (ALA) (2018), outreach programming (1) encourages users to utilize library services, and (2) encourages librarians to design programs targeted to an underserved or inadequately serviced user group. The ALA supports, and even recommends, that all libraries develop and maintain outreach policies and guidelines for library roles in services to diverse groups of students. Further supporting this, the Association of College and Research Libraries (ACRL), a division of ALA, created the ACRL Value of Academic Libraries Statement in 2016. This document lists four important criteria for academic libraries' work with students: (1) support student success, (2) promote student achievement, (3) foster student learning, and (4) improve the student experience. Academic libraries work hard to accomplish all of these things with all students through outreach activities and initiatives. Carter and Seaman (2011) identified two categories of outreach—providing services and promotion of services. Services were listed as (1) assistance with research or information, (2) resources available at the library, and (3) library facilities. Promoting these services is done through a variety of library marketing methods. In previous chapters we addressed improving services by discussing how to adjust the library's physical environment, references services, and instruction to better serve students with ASD. In this chapter, we will focus on promoting our services to students with ASD, which supports the ACRL core value criteria listed above. Promotion of services is especially important with this particular group of students. Due to the characteristics we have discussed throughout this book, including communication and executive functioning difficulties, students with ASD are less likely to take the initiative to seek out services on their own. Academic libraries should absolutely make an effort to get involved with ASD programs and support students with ASD on campus as it will have a positive impact on the overall success and outcome of these students at college.

THE NEED FOR ASD AWARENESS

When asked what they desired to succeed in college, the greatest self-reported need of students with ASD is autism or neurodiversity awareness on college campuses (Sarrett 2017; Van Hees, Moyson, and Roeyers 2015). Many students report a lack of understanding or inaccurate perceptions of autism spectrum disorder (Van Hees, Moyson, and Roeyers 2015). Increasing awareness of ASD on campuses allows room for successful transitions of students with ASD to college in two ways. First, it helps foster an atmosphere on campus where students feel accepted and welcome. Second, when faculty and staff are knowledgeable about ASD, it increases the success of services provided by disability support offices and other offices across campus (including the library). Ideally, training should be made available to all employees and students on campus. This includes awareness of traits and characteristics of ASD as well as educational practices such as Universal Design and academic accommodations (Sarrett 2017). Promoting acceptance and support for college students with ASD will have an overall positive impact in the campus community. Achieving this level of acceptance may require "transforming a campus community's broader culture" because of the fact that the needs of students with ASD are different from other groups on campus (Robertson and Ne'eman 2008). When awareness and training are done properly, students with ASD will feel accepted and supported, which will make them more successful in college. Additionally, neurotypical students on campus will be more understanding and thoughtful when working and socializing with students with ASD.

Academic librarians absolutely have an important role to play in this process. Student success continues to increase for those with ASD when there is positive and ongoing collaboration between classroom faculty and campus supports like librarians and library staff (Knott and Taylor 2014; Sosnowy, Silverman, and Shattuck 2017). College students with ASD in particular "require support for both academic and *non-academic aspects* of the college experience throughout their years in higher education" (Robertson and Ne'eman 2008). We have placed emphasis in the quotation on "non-academic aspects," because this is an area where students with ASD are very different from other groups of students. As we have discussed before, individuals with ASD often have trouble understanding the unwritten rules of society—they must consciously learn these rules that come naturally to most neurotypical students. Unfortunately, there is no such thing as a "common curriculum of skills necessary in adulthood" that can serve as a set of rules for students with ASD to navigate college, which makes having support in college essential for them (Schall, Wheman, and Carr 2014). Relevant and timely academic and nonacademic support has been found to decrease the anxiety of students with ASD while increasing their success (Cai and Richdale 2016). The benefits of college ASD programs that are successful in providing this support include not only increased retention rates but even greater success of students in employment post-bachelor's (Barnhill 2016). By introducing the library into the support system of students with ASD through outreach and programming, students will have a better college experience and overall higher success rates (Hendrickson et al. 2017). This is an excellent opportunity for libraries to play a pivotal role in developing awareness and support for students with ASD in their own libraries and across campus.

ACADEMIC ACCOMMODATIONS AND SUPPORTS FOR STUDENTS WITH ASD

Since many students with ASD have had high levels of academic and social supports in their primary and secondary years of school, this has resulted in increased enrollment in higher education in recent years. As noted in the introduction of this book, enrollment is occurring at a fast rate and will continue to grow. However, the scholarly literature has not caught up in identifying the appropriate and most effective methods of support in higher education. The result is that colleges and universities are currently underprepared to offer appropriate supports for students with ASD to transition into college and succeed throughout their college career (Cox et al. 2017). In this chapter, we will address several different types of supports: academic accommodations, academic supports, and nonacademic supports. Academic accommodations are offered through the Office of Disability Services at any college or university and are a legally binding contract of specific services that must be followed by professors and other personnel. Academic supports are considered specific campus offerings a student must approach for help such as tutoring, the writing center, and the library. Nonacademic supports, discussed in the next section, include social and emotional supports found across campus.

Some, but not all, college students with ASD will qualify for academic accommodations. As we previously mentioned in Chapter 4 on instruction, academic accommodations are not available automatically in higher education institutions. In order to receive specialized academic accommodations, any college student with a disability must self-disclose his or her disability to the Office of Disability Services. If a student chooses to do so, a letter of accommodation is given to the student for them to present to offices, teaching faculty, and any pertinent campus contacts or programs. This document does not disclose the student's disability. It only specifically outlines accommodations that should be followed (e.g., extended test-taking time). It is up to the student to disclose their disability if they choose to do so. The trouble with this process is that it requires college students to both self-disclose and self-advocate. Many college students, including those with ASD, simply do not want to self-disclose. A big part of this hesitation is the fear of being stigmatized (Anderson, Stephenson, and Carter 2017; Cai and Richdale 2016; Knott and Taylor 2014). Many students with ASD attend college to experience a normal life situation and do not want to draw attention to their disability or a need for supports or services (Cox et al. 2017;

Knott and Taylor 2014; Van Hees, Moyson, and Roeyers 2015). The problem is, if they do not seek out supports and services, they are much less likely to succeed in college.

New college students may also have a hard time with the need to advocate for themselves. All of their educational career prior to college has been led by parents, teachers, and school administrators. However, once they go to college, they are now expected to manage all aspects of their education on their own. This sudden requirement for self-advocacy applies both to the formal process of seeking out academic accommodations, or other types of campus supports, and also to many other processes that a student must face on campus such as registering for classes, communicating with the financial aid office, or using the library. Given that students with ASD have poor self-advocacy and social skills and may not have had much experience self-advocating in the past, it is doubly difficult for them to approach an unfamiliar location or unfamiliar people, disclose their disability, and communicate their need for support. Even the first step of "identifying supportive people in a new environment" may be very challenging for them (White et al. 2017). As an example, for a student with ASD, even the act of approaching service desks in an academic library requires self-advocacy. There can be one service desk or many; there may be one library on campus or several. Knowing how, when, and where to ask for assistance in the library can be confusing. Both the hesitation of students with ASD to self-disclose and their limited experience with self-advocacy reinforce the idea that outreach on the part of the library is especially essential for this group.

Problems with self-advocacy can lead to serious problems for students with ASD. For instance, in Anderson, Carter, and Stephenson's 2018 study, results showed that many academic supports and services were often not utilized by students with ASD. The main reason was the "lack of follow up by disability services" (Anderson, Carter, and Stephenson 2018). In other words, students with ASD will not "just ask" for the help they need. Therefore, it is necessary that offices and programs with services consistently follow up or reach out to initiate and grow communication with the students who need the services. This is an extremely important lesson for academic libraries. This is not a case where students will come to us. We must make the effort to not only develop services to help students with ASD but to then make connections with those students so that they are comfortable enough to use those services. Benefits include improved socialization, increased independence, life skills, and high academic achievement (Anderson, Stephenson, and Carter 2017). The more that students with ASD make use of supports and services, the more likely they are to be successful in college!

In a recent study academic supports were nominated as the most helpful support in college by students with ASD (Anderson, Carter, and Stephenson 2018). Unfortunately, the library is often not mentioned as an academic support in studies regarding students with ASD in higher education. The scholarly literature addresses advising, mentoring, tutoring, test-taking assistance, life skills, social skills instruction, and employment assistance, but not the library (Barnhill 2016; Sosnowy, Silverman, and Shattuck 2017)! This gap in the research demonstrates a clear need for academic libraries to become more involved in the support system of this student population. Given these results, and given that libraries consider themselves to play an important role in the academic success of students, the library can be considered an academic support—it is especially important that librarians and staff find ways to reach out to students with ASD.

NONACADEMIC SUPPORTS FOR STUDENTS WITH ASD

At most colleges and universities, students with ASD are accepted based on their academic qualifications just as any other student. They are intellectually capable of all the academic demands a college or university has to offer. This is great news because, overall, success in college is directly related to academic achievement in higher education (Nasamran, Witmer, and Los 2017). However, although students with ASD may be ready for college academically, social skills are also a significant predictor of success in higher education and employment after college (Nasamran, Witmer, and Los 2017). Although academic supports, such as tutoring or writing centers, are readily available in college, nonacademic supports, such as social and emotional support, are more difficult to identify and are not often available as a support in college (Cullen 2015). Given that social and emotional traits tend to be areas that give students with ASD a lot of difficulty or anxiety, it can present a challenge to find and approach these services in college.

In a 2015 study, Cullen found that the three main ways that students with ASD received social interaction were with family, friends, and through social media. At face value, this does not sound too different from most college students. Family, however, was the primary social interaction for students with ASD who lived both on and off campus. This is probably not the case for most neurotypical students, especially those living on campus. Only about half of the students studied reported they met friends through classes or social gatherings on campus, in particular, events sponsored by the college or university that facilitated social interactions for students with ASD. Even though some students with ASD are meeting people and making friends through campus events, it is still a difficult thing for them to do. In a more recent study of college students with autism (Jackson et al. 2018), participants were found to actually have a hard time "integrating with the broader campus environment." If students with ASD have trouble making friends in person, they may fall back on social media as a method of socialization because it reduces the anxiety component of interacting or communicating with others in person (Van Hees, Moyson, and Roeyers 2015).

Persons with ASD often feel lonely and are aware of their difficulties with social communication (Knott and Taylor 2014; Robledo, Donnellan, and Strandt-Conroy 2012; Sayman 2015; Schriber, Robins, and Solomon 2014; Van Hees, Moyson, and Roeyers 2015). Offering a variety of opportunities for them to successfully navigate peer groups in college reduces anxiety, increases satisfaction, and also social acceptance overall (Cullen 2015; LeGary 2017). Any opportunity for social interaction and experiences increases the overall positive college experience of a student with ASD. It also gives them the skills necessary to interact in many different situations in college and beyond, especially employment situations. What does all this mean for academic libraries and those who work within them? It means we need to think beyond research help and instruction. Although research assistance and library instruction support the academic needs of students with autism, they do not address their social needs which, as we have seen, is the more significant need to address through support. When programs and outreach offer social opportunities for students with ASD, it increases their involvement in extracurricular activities and increases variety in peer relationships (Ashbaugh, Koegel, and Koegel 2017). This also results in increased academic performance and overall increased level of satisfaction with the college experience (Ashbaugh, Koegel, and Koegel 2017). This is something that libraries can do! Given that many students with ASD do in fact meet friends through organized campus activities but continue to find it hard to do, the library can certainly become another location or host of social gatherings for diverse groups of students.

THE ROLE OF THE ACADEMIC LIBRARY IN ACADEMIC AND NONACADEMIC SUPPORTS

Academic libraries easily support the academic skills of all students through individual and class instruction sessions. Incorporating the strategies and tips provided in Chapters 3 and 4 will support students with ASD specifically. We also have the ability to support students socially as well. Strategies for outreach and support will vary depending on if your institution has an autism support program and how active the program is. If your institution does not have a specific program, you can still facilitate a relationship through your campus's Office of Disability Services, counseling services, or any other campus office that is working closely with these students.

Recent studies conducted surveys of college students with autism spectrum disorder to evaluate the need and use of accommodations and services at colleges as well as outcomes of using these services (Hillier et al. 2017; Sosnowy, Silverman, and Shattuck 2017). The studies noted that many institutions in higher education are still lacking in specific supports or accommodations for ASD, yet these programs can be easily implemented. For institutions that have programs or supports, outcomes indicated reduced loneliness, increased self-esteem, and lower anxiety (Hillier et al. 2017). One participant of the Sosnowy, Silverman, and Shattuck (2017) study who attended a college with a well-established autism support program, reported having great success at college due to the "broad range of programs and services, including academic support, mentorship, social groups, life skills classes, and summer programs." The participant also described staff as understanding and accepting of autism and that she felt very comfortable at this particular institution because of the appropriate supports that were in place. West Chester University's DCAP Autism Program, and the relationship the library has with this program, serves as an excellent example of the types of programming and support that can be in place at a college or university. Our experience and success conducting outreach and working with DCAP forms the basis for many of our suggestions in the remainder of this chapter.

STUDENT VOICES

I am also extremely involved in our Autism Support Program on campus. They have really helped me find a happy and safe place to be. I feel like they actually want to spend time with me. It's a place I can be myself. I would encourage students to reach out and utilize their supports.

—**Emma Billingsley**

In Sarrett's 2017 study, participants revealed a need for more opportunities to improve the social life of students with autism spectrum disorder and the availability of support groups and structured activities for predictable social interactions. The study suggests scheduling campus activities and events on a regular schedule and in a designated, neurodiverse space (see Chapter 2 for an explanation of neurodiverse spaces). As much as possible, the space should be free of too many sensory interferences that might not provide a comfortable place for students with ASD. Many libraries are well suited to host social gatherings or activities, because we have a variety of physical spaces and flexibility in available hours.

Support programs designed to build social skills or networks would improve the college experience of students with ASD (Scott Jackson et al. 2018). The more students with ASD who have opportunities to interact with others, the more successful they will be in college and in the workforce. "To allow students to succeed, it is clear that support needs to encompass more than academic skills" (Knott and Taylor 2014). Students with ASD need more than academic supports, and libraries need to be a part of that support structure. Reach out and get involved!

Going to the Program

If your campus does have a specific autism support program, this is an obvious starting point for outreach. According to Barnhill's (2016) study, high numbers of college students with ASD enrolled in a specific ASD program on campus utilize the program's services. In fact, 40 percent of the programs surveyed reported an enrollment rate of 100 percent of students with ASD. Even more impressive is that 30 percent of programs surveyed reported that 75 to 99 percent of students with ASD accessed the services available to them through the program. These are tremendous numbers. If there is a specific ASD program on your campus, these numbers indicate that any outreach and collaboration will positively impact the enrolled students. Libraries have a great opportunity to get involved and create outreach initiatives to help support and collaborate with the campus ASD programs. The authors did just that when our own campus autism support program, DCAP, was established.

Instead of waiting for your campus program to reach out to the library, you should initiate contact with college services and programs that support students with ASD. College employees in these offices and programs are often extremely busy orienting and supporting their student participants in addition to the day-to-day routines of the university work. As we discussed above, the library is not appearing in the scholarly literature as a potential partner in campus ASD programs. It probably is not even occurring to the directors and administrators of these programs that the library is a possible valuable and positive campus connection. By taking initiative and getting in touch with these offices with specific ideas for collaboration, you are more likely to experience success with your outreach. Visiting the program's office on campus, especially when the students are there, is an excellent first step. This will make the students feel more comfortable and give them a visual cue (facial recognition) that when they are in the library and see you, they know you are someone who can help.

Developing an Outreach Plan

There are many ways an academic library can conduct outreach to students with ASD. Although it is easiest if there is a campus program to work directly with, this does not account for the students who choose to not disclose that they have ASD. Therefore, we suggest a two-pronged approach—outreach targeted to autism programs while at the same time marketing to the whole campus or through the Office of Disability Services. This will increase the chance that more students with ASD will see and benefit from your outreach initiatives. Furthermore, because "outreach works best when there is ongoing management," providing occasional or inconsistent outreach and programming creates services barriers (Brannen, Milewski, and Mack 2017). Once you start, try to be consistent. Creating an outreach plan to follow, assess, and build on is important. Consider meeting with library administration to include library services for students with diverse needs, students with ASD among them, in the library's mission or strategic plan. Once it is part of the strategic plan, it is a good idea to also make it part of the library's marketing plan so that students and programs are aware of the library's efforts, resources, and services for students with autism.

The desired outcome in all outreach is to make the students feel comfortable and welcome. We want them to visit or use the library and its services. Demonstrating practical tips, showing that librarians are more than encyclopedias and reference desks, and explaining the usefulness of particular library resources like databases will make the students feel welcome and comfortable. It is even more essential to be approachable and engaging in all outreach. For librarians that are the liaisons to ASD programs or staff that have been trained in autism awareness, use an indicator for offices that shows it is an autism friendly space or personnel.

Following are specific strategies for outreach to students with autism spectrum disorder or a campus autism program.

Strategies

LibGuides, Web Pages, and Handouts

Use these methods to promote services and spaces that may be conducive to students with ASD. Make sure accessibility of any documents, web pages, materials, etc. is a priority. Provide these materials in a variety of formats (video, audio, PDF, etc.) so that different types of learners can access them and use them. This demonstrates a sign of support from the library. It also makes navigating a new situation easier for students with autism since they do not have to ask for assistance in person. Flyers or handouts should be distributed to program offices. The authors, at the suggestion of our program director Cherie, created a handout for the students in the program that noted specific service locations (Appendix B). In this and all material, we try to use visuals or pictures as much as possible since students with ASD are visual learners. We took pictures of all the service points and included them in the handout. If you have a campus program, make sure you provide them with extra copies—our program keeps resources like this in a special binder that is easily accessible to all students enrolled in the program.

TIPS FROM OUR EXPERT: RESOURCE BINDER

Cherie Fishbaugh, MA, BCBA, BS-L (PA)

As resources are shared with the students, it is crucial to centralize the information. A campus resource binder is located at our autism program office. The binder consists of the different resources across campus. In the library section one will find a photo directory of library staff including how they can help, a task analysis of how to access resources, what resources are available, and a tips sheet consisting of hours, ideal times to get a quiet area, and quiet floors.

In the near future, the authors have plans to make a LibGuide specific to our local autism program, which will include handouts and other specialized information about the library and its services that we think students with ASD should know, such as a list of librarians who have attended autism training, good study locations, and how to obtain specific library services.

Orientations or Tours

This is one of the first things that we did when our campus autism support program began and we have continued to do each year. Tours or orientations to the library building are extremely important because they give students with ASD the opportunity to familiarize themselves with the building layout and the location of specific offices (Polger and Sheidlower 2017). Schedule a quiet time and space for students in an ASD program (or students who have self-identified through the Office of Disability Services), to come and meet librarians and visit the library space. We schedule these "socials" on Friday afternoons when the library is generally less crowded and quieter. This is a learning as well as a much-needed social opportunity where students with ASD have the chance to navigate a new situation, communicate with others, and learn something new. Plus, meeting at least one or two librarians gives them someone they already know whom they can seek out for help later. During the tour, point out and explain specific service desks. In addition to a tour, take some time to introduce the library website, demonstrate library databases, and point out helpful resources such as chat services. At the suggestion of our program director, we ask each student what his or her major is and then show the corresponding LibGuide as a way to introduce the students to "their librarian." As discussed in Chapter 2, people with ASD can find large spaces overwhelming and difficult to navigate, which increases anxiety behaviors. Having opportunities to see and explore a space in a structured and supportive way will increase the likelihood that the student will come back to use the library in a more successful way. Before our first tour, we actually took the time to walk through our library, keeping in mind environmental sensitivities such as lighting and noise. This allowed us to make suggestions for where students might want to go for certain types of study areas—especially areas that tend to be quieter and have natural light. Rule-based, structured activities provide students an opportunity to learn how to interact with their peers or campus professionals and staff (Knott and Taylor 2014). For this reason, it is recommended that tours are not self-guided but rather led by a professional librarian with training in working with students with ASD. Having a structured tour and information session allows time for students to process each area in the library.

TIPS FROM OUR EXPERT: COLLABORATING WITH THE LIBRARY

Cherie Fishbaugh, MA, BCBA, BS-L (PA)

As a director of autism services, it is critical to collaborate with other resources across campus, especially the library. Many students with autism find comfort in the library; it's one of the few areas that stays consistent from high school to college. However, when transitioning to a campus, anxiety of entering new places can become overwhelming. It is extremely helpful to introduce the students to the library staff as well as to have a tour. During this "meet and greet" opportunity, the staff build rapport with students, point out the quiet areas, discuss and demonstrate how to access resources, and give helpful tips to best utilize the resources.

Another aspect of the "socials" is that we provide food. The presence of food shifts the experience from an educational experience to a social experience. After the tour and presentation, we take some time to talk to the students while everyone enjoys the snacks. Our program director uses this as an opportunity to discuss the appropriate social rules for this type of interaction with the students ahead of time and then models that behavior during the event.

Displays and Exhibits

Displays and exhibits are a common and effective outreach activity. They can take on multiple roles, including increasing awareness and acceptance on campus and advertising the campus autism program. Highlight students with autism and information about autism spectrum disorder in a positive way. This is an excellent way to connect students with ASD to their campus community as a whole. If a display coincides with a particular campus event or national recognition such as Autism Awareness Month in April, the library can use the opportunity to host the campus autism program for a social or gathering. Put books on display about autism that can be checked out as well as informational sheets or bookmarks for people to take. The authors had the fortunate opportunity to work with a graduate assistant (GA) from the DCAP program on such a display (see Thoughts from Our Expert below for more information). In fact, she reached out to us to collaborate on an exhibit about autism awareness during Autism Awareness Month in April. The GA developed the theme and the look of the display, and we developed a list of materials, pulling items the library owned and ordering materials that we found would benefit the collection. The relationship we established early on by reaching out to the autism program at its onset went a long way to the reciprocity in working together on future initiatives.

THOUGHTS FROM OUR EXPERT: COLLABORATING WITH THE LIBRARY

Cherie Fishbaugh, MA, BCBA, BS-L (PA)

The opportunity to provide trainings and to work directly with the library staff has led the efforts of building an inclusive campus community. There is an increased effort to raise awareness, knowledge, and acceptance across the campus. The library has purchased books and materials to educate others on autism. During autism awareness month, they created a display "The Power of Neurodiversity: Autism Unveiled" featuring people with autism from authors to actors, beauty queens to artists, and our university's own alumni, graduate students, and undergraduate students. The display grabbed the attention of our campus population and resulted in all but a few autism-related books being checked out. We are a campus of more than 17,000 students, and with continuous collaboration we raise awareness, understanding, and acceptance of our neurodiverse students.

Short Instruction or Information Sessions

Although many college classes have the opportunity for formal library research instruction (discussed in Chapter 4), offering shorter instruction or information sessions in an informal and relaxed setting will make students with ASD more comfortable and provide them the opportunity to ask questions and practice information literacy skills. These can be coupled with the orientation or tour, as we did, or offered separately.

Host an Event

The library is an excellent venue to host autism awareness events such as discussions or film screenings. Invite a student and/or expert panel to

SELECT LIST OF FILMS ABOUT AUTISM SPECTRUM DISORDER:

The United States of Autism (2013)

Temple Grandin (2010)

Autism: The Musical (2008)

We're All in This Together: Understanding the Humanity of Autism (2010)

Breaking Boundaries: The Art of Alex Masket (2009)

The Changing Face of Autism (2008)

A Time for Georgia (1970)

The Red Kite Project: A Documentary (2011)

JJ's Journey: A Journey about Autism (2008)

George (2000)

A Mother's Courage: Talking Back to Autism (2013)

Sounding the Alarm: Battling the Autism Epidemic (2014)

speak about the experiences of college students on the autism spectrum and provide a question-and-answer component for open dialogue. For newly published books or articles on autism awareness or information about students with ASD attending college, host a book or resource discussion session. Hosting a film screening can be a popular event, and there are many great films to choose from. Utilizing the library's available streaming resources is a great way to do this inexpensively. If in the library's means, paying for performance rights for more popular films is another option. All of these ideas are a great way to offer another opportunity for students to interact socially.

Workshops

Team up with career services, counseling offices, the writing center, or other relevant campus resources to offer professional development workshops. Although the focus could be on how to prepare for employment, how to be a good employee, finding internships, etc., there could also be a social focus where the workshop provides another opportunity for a student with ASD to interact with others. The library often has access to career resources and databases and other relevant resources.

Office Hours at the Program

If your college or university is lucky enough to have an autism program on campus, an excellent way to build rapport with the program would be to hold regularly scheduled hours at the program site. During this time you can assist with research help, answer other library-related questions, and also provide an opportunity for social interaction with the students. This will hopefully lead them to become more comfortable with seeking out help in the library.

Mentorship

Offer to be a mentor to a student with autism. Many studies (Gillespie-Lynch et al. 2017; Sarrett 2017; Thompson et al. 2018) point to the success of peer and professional mentoring for students with ASD. Mentors can assist with both academic and social skills including self-advocacy. Mentors should be trained in autism or neurodiversity awareness before applying to be a mentor.

Collection Development

Obtain current materials and resources on autism spectrum disorder including books, DVDs, and streaming content. Materials should cover everything from defining autism spectrum disorder to college personnel working with people with ASD, anecdotal and narrative materials, popular and documentary films on ASD, as well as scholarly resources (Longtin 2014). Acquiring materials on ASD demonstrates the library's supportive role and ability to participate in raising awareness and advocating for students with ASD.

Student Involvement

Have student members of the program participate in outreach directly. Students with ASD would like more awareness and understanding. Including them in the outreach process gives them the voice and opportunity to help increase awareness. They can assist in creating educational materials, hosting events, selecting appropriate materials, and even teaching outreach classes. This provides a model of inclusion and an excellent example to other students that the library is a supportive and inclusive place on campus.

Swag and Food

In all outreach and programming opportunities, it is important to have library swag. Useful items with important contact information such as pens, flash drives, and highlighters are popular items. Of course, no library event would be complete without food! This provides a social opportunity and time to informally chat with the students.

It is always important to remember that autism is a spectrum and each student falls on the spectrum differently. Strategies and outreach programs that work well for one student may not work well for another. Providing a variety of outreach methods and opportunities is important. Think creatively and outside the box to find ways to share and teach the library's resources.

Library Staff Training

The library, as the center of academic learning, should take a . . . role on college and university campuses in training their faculty and staff to provide the best possible service. Enriching the library performance for persons with disabilities will impact instruction, outreach, inclusion, and awareness in general. These efforts . . . will enhance the university experience of people with disabilities. (Brannen, Milewski, and Mack 2017)

The above quote is especially pertinent regarding working with students with ASD. Lack of awareness and knowledge about autism spectrum disorder from college faculty and staff hinders the integration and success of students with ASD into the college environment (Barnard-Brak, Lechtenberger, and Lan 2010; Barnhill 2016; Cherney 2017; LeGary 2017). By providing regular training to library personnel including student workers, the library will create a positive, supportive environment for students with ASD. This can also serve as a model for other departments and offices on campus.

In order to remain effective and efficient at the point of need in the library, employees should participate in periodic training. All library personnel including student workers, security guards, and administration should have the opportunity to participate. Consider providing flexible types of training or multiple training times for staff that work in the evening or at night. Also, it is extremely important to repeat training on a regular basis or make it a routine part of the new hiring process. Library staff can change frequently, especially student workers. The idea is to make all patrons comfortable, regardless if they have a disability or not. However, staff training specific to disabilities enables better service for patrons and an overall more positive experience using the library.

Ideally, collaborative training with the Office of Disability Services or a campus autism support program can be provided. If this is not possible, reach out to a community resource that may be willing to come in to provide information and/or training. Training should include informing library staff about the population including the characteristics and traits of ASD; discussion topics about college students with ASD; training that focuses on etiquette and communication guidelines so that library staff interact with students with ASD effectively; specific examples and/or role-playing training is ideal.

In order to offer the greatest opportunity for training to all library personnel, utilizing different types of training might be a good idea.

- Live training in the library with experienced campus professionals or outside experts. This is the best choice as it offers an opportunity for question-and-answer sessions and possibly training where interactions can be modeled.

- Web training modules: This may be useful for student workers, as well as staff that work in the evening or nighttime hours. Training modules can be used as assessment strategies to indicate increased awareness among staff interacting with students with ASD.

CONCLUSION

As outreach and programming are implemented, set goals and objectives. This will help measure the success of specific initiatives and actions (Salamon 2016). It is important to assess and measure the success of any outreach program so that challenges can be addressed and to continue building on what is successful.

One of the challenges of outreach is that it requires a considerable amount of time, staff, sustainability, and even financial support (Salamon 2016).

Creating a library outreach position specifically for services and programs to people with disabilities is an excellent option if financially available. If your library is not able to do this, establishing a librarian who can be the liaison with the Office of Disability Services or a specific autism program on campus will increase support for the population, especially in terms of a partnerships with the library (Brannen, Milewski, and Mack 2017). If neither of these are possible, a library committee can always be formed to share the outreach responsibilities and help brainstorm ideas, run trainings, and collaborate with appropriate groups, students, and/or campus offices. Committee members should include library departmental representatives including electronic resources, instruction, public services, assessment, student success, etc. This helps the library make comprehensive recommendations for services to students with ASD but also ensures that these departments are aware any issues, concerns, or initiatives (Brannen, Milewski, and Mack 2017).

Constantly collect feedback from the departments or programs you are working with so as to evaluate and ultimately improve services. Although academic libraries are big on gathering data and statistics to measure successes and failures, it is also important to gather evaluations from students who have been directly impacted by any outreach or programming. If there is an autism support program, deliver an electronic survey to the students for anecdotal and observational feedback. This is just as important as the numerical data. Additionally, your own observations and thoughts as you implement and conduct outreach are important. Take a few minutes to write up a brief review from your own perspective of any event, social, gathering, display, etc. so that you have a review of what worked and what did not work for future programming. Reflecting on your own work is just as important as the reflection of those attending. Together the data, evaluations from participants, and your own evaluations provide a valuable picture of the outreach initiative as a whole.

Remember that the outcome of any outreach or program initiative may not have immediate measurable success or outcomes. There is an investment of time to form relationships and grow an idea and initiative into something exciting. Do not get discouraged by failures or things that do not work. Instead, focus on the small successes and positive results and build off of those while finding ways to change or modify the parts that did not work. By doing this, outreach programming will be a rewarding investment.

STUDENT VOICES

I believe I have many strengths, more than I had last year. As I conclude my first year of college I would say my strengths include: self-advocacy, focus on self and health, learning more about positive relationships, and continue to be involved with many organizations/activities on campus and within the community.—**Emma Billingsley**

RECOMMENDED READING

Brannen, Michelle H., Steven Milewski, and Thura Mack. 2017. "Providing Staff Training and Programming to Support People with Disabilities: An Academic Library Case Study." *Public Services Quarterly* 13, no. 2: 61–77. https://doi.org/10.1080/15228959.2017.1298491.

> This is one of the only articles that specifically addresses academic library outreach to support students with disabilities. It is a case study that has an excellent literature review and provides practical advice for outreach and training that is applicable to students with ASD.

Longtin, Susan E. 2014. "Using the College Infrastructure to Support Students on the Autism Spectrum." *Journal of Postsecondary Education and Disability* 27, no. 1: 63–72. https://eric.ed.gov/?id=EJ10 29568.

> Although this article covers many different college offices or programs that could support students with ASD, one of those included is the library! This is very exciting as most literature does not include the library as a campus support.

Sarrett, Jennifer. 2017. "Autism and Accommodations in Higher Education: Insights from the Autism Community." *Journal of Autism and Developmental Disorders* 48, no. 3: 679–693. https://doi.org/10.1007/s10803-017-3353-4.

> Sarrett's article covers accommodations for students with ASD in detail. Additionally, she writes about many important aspects of students with ASD in higher education settings including campus awareness and training, Universal Design, inclusion, and social outreach by studying the experiences of students with ASD in college.

Van Hees, Valérie, Tinneke Moyson, and Herbert Roeyers. 2015. "Higher Education Experiences of Students with Autism Spectrum Disorder:

Challenges, Benefits and Support Needs." *Journal of Autism & Developmental Disorders* 45, no. 6: 1673–1688. https://doi.org/10 .1007/s10803-014-2324-2.

A group of students with ASD were studied to determine challenges they meet in attending college as well as their needs for support. Van Hees, Moyson, and Roeyers provide concrete recommendations for support based on the challenges that can be applied to outreach initiatives through the library.

APPENDIX A

HANDOUT FOR LIBRARY EMPLOYEES

WORKING WITH STUDENTS WITH AUTISM SPECTRUM DISORDER (ASD)

The prevalence rate of ASD among 18 year olds is 1 in 88.

Keep in mind: Not every person with ASD has every characteristic described below. They are all individuals with their own strengths and weaknesses!

Common Characteristics:

- Communication
    - Tone (speech may seem flat or stilted)
    - Volume (may not be appropriate to situation)
    - Body language (may seem stiff, may not make eye contact)
    - May misinterpret nonliteral language
- Behavior
    - May have trouble interpreting social cues
    - May not know/understand unwritten rules of behavior
    - May show repetitive behaviors
- Organization
    - May have difficulty adapting to change
    - May have trouble organizing time or materials
    - May need help shifting from one task to another

Common Positive Characteristics:

- Honest and straightforward
- Open-minded and fair
- Love of learning
- Original and creative thinkers
- Great attention to detail

Tips:

- Use literal language (avoid figures of speech, irony, sarcasm)
- Explain the rules (especially social/behavior rules)
- Provide short, specific instructions
- Provide concrete examples
- Use visuals/graphics when possible
- Set clear expectations

APPENDIX B

HANDOUT TO HELP STUDENTS NAVIGATE THE LIBRARY

F. H. GREEN LIBRARY

Where to go for help

If You Need . . .

→ RESEARCH HELP, go to . . .

Research Help Desk (best bet on campus)	main floor, near the entrance
Chat interface (best bet off campus)	library homepage, tab on right
Your librarian (best for upper-level classes)	http://library.wcupa.edu/ask/subject

→ QUIET STUDY SPACE, go to . . .

Main floor quiet study room	Turn left when entering, room past computers
4th, 5th, 6th floors	Higher the quieter, no natural light on 6th

TIP: Nights = noisy! Early mornings and weekend afternoons are the quietest times.

→ SPACE TO WORK WITH FRIENDS/CLASSMATES, go to . . .

Group computer rooms   RM 252 and RM 253 (253 coming soon)

Lower level near Starbucks   Noisiest

Rest of lower level   Fairly noisy

West side of main floor   People talk, but not as noisy

→ TO CHECK OUT A BOOK OR A BOOK ON RESERVE, go to . . .

Library Help Desk   Directly across from the main entrance

→ COLOR PRINTING OR POSTER PRINTING OR TO BORROW A LAPTOP, go to . . .

IMC (instructional media center desk)   lower level, across from elevators

→ CAFFEINE OR SUGAR, go to . . .

Starbucks   Separate entrance, or from lower level by noisiest study area

Vending machines   Lower level, hidden in journals area

References

American Library Association (ALA). 2009. "Services to Persons with Disabilities: An Interpretation of the Library Bill of Rights." http://www.ala.org/advocacy/intfreedom/librarybill/interpretations/servicespeopledisabilities.

American Library Association (ALA). 2018. "ALA's Office of Literacy & Outreach Services: Supporting the Libraries of Underserved Populations." http://www.ala.org/aboutala/offices/olos/ortips.

American Psychiatric Association (APA). 2013. *Diagnostic and Statistical Manual of Mental Disorders,* 5th ed. (DSM-5). Arlington, VA.: American Psychiatric Association.

Anderson, Anastasia H., Mark Carter, and Jennifer Stephenson. 2018. "Perspectives of University Students with Autism Spectrum Disorder." *Journal of Autism and Developmental Disorders* 48: 651–665. https://doi.org/10.1007/s10803-017-3257-3.

Anderson, Anastasia H., Jennifer Stephenson, and Mark Carter. 2017. "A Systematic Literature Review of the Experiences and Supports of Students with Autism Spectrum Disorder in Post-Secondary Education." *Research in Autism Spectrum Disorders* 39: 33–53. http://dx.doi.org/10.1016/j.rasd.2017.04.002.

Asaro-Saddler, Kristie. 2016. "Using Evidence-Based Practices to Teach Writing to Children with Autism Spectrum Disorders." *Preventing School Failure* 60, no. 1: 79–85. https://doi.org/10.1080/1045988X.2014.981793.

Ashbaugh, Kristen, Robert L. Koegel, and Lynn Kern Koegel. 2017. "Increasing Social Integration for College Students with Autism Spectrum Disorder." *Behavioral Development Bulletin* 22, no. 1: 183–196. https://doi.org/10.1037/bdb0000057.

Association of College & Research Libraries (ACRL). 2012. "Diversity Standards: Cultural Competency for Academic Libraries." http://www.ala.org/acrl/standards/diversity.

Association of College & Research Libraries (ACRL). 2015. "Framework for Information Literacy for Higher Education." http://www.ala.org/acrl/standards/ilframework.

Association of College & Research Libraries (ACRL). 2016. "Value of Academic Libraries Statement." https://acrl.ala.org/value/wp-content/uploads/2016/07/Value-of-Academic-Libraries-Statement-FINAL.pdf.

Association of Specialized and Cooperative Library Agencies (ASCLA). 2006. "Library Services for People with Disabilities Policy." http://www.ala.org/ascla/resources/libraryservices.

Baldwin, Susanna, Debra Costley, and Anthony Warren. 2014. "Employment Activities and Experiences of Adults with High-Functioning Autism and Asperger's Disorder." *Journal of Autism and Developmental Disorders* 44, no. 10: 2440–2449. https://doi.org/10.1007/s10803-014-2112-z.

Banerjee, Robin. 2006. "Executive Function." In *Encyclopaedic Dictionary of Psychology*, ed. Graham Davey. London: Hodder Arnold.

Barnard-Brak, Lucy, DeAnn Lechtenberger, and William Y. Lan. 2010. "Accommodation Strategies of College Students with Disabilities." *Qualitative Report* 15, no. 2: 411–429. http://www.nova.edu/ssss/QR/QR15-2/barnard-brak.pdf

Barnhill, Gena P. 2016. "Supporting Students with Asperger Syndrome on College Campuses." *Focus on Autism and Other Developmental Disabilities* 31, no. 1: 3–15. https://doi.org/10.1177/1088357614523121.

Basken, Paul. 2017. "Colleges Are Trying a Broad Approach to Autistic Students. What Will that Cost?" *The Chronicle of Higher Education* 64, no. 3: A30. https://www.chronicle.com/article/Colleges-Are-Trying-a-Broad/241027.

Blaska, Joan. 1993. "The Power of Language: Speak and Write Using 'Person First.'" In *Perspectives on Disability: Text and Readings on Disability*, ed. Mark Nagler. Palo Alto, CA: Health Markets Research.

Bogdashina, Olga. 2004. *Communication Issues in Autism and Asperger Syndrome: Do We Speak the Same Language?* London: Jessica Kingsley.

Brannen, Michelle H., Steven Milewski, and Thura Mack. 2017. "Providing Staff Training and Programming to Support People with Disabilities: An Academic Library Case Study." *Public Services Quarterly* 13, no. 2: 61–77. https://doi.org/10.1080/15228959.2017.1298491.

Brown, Lydia. 2011a. "The Significance of Semantics: Person-First Language: Why It Matters." *Autistic Hoya.* Accessed September 11, 2017. http://www.thinkingautismguide.com/2011/11/person-first-language-why-it-matters.html.

Brown, Lydia. 2011b. "Identity and Hypocrisy: A Second Argument against Person-First Language." *Autistic Hoya.* Accessed September 11, 2017. https://www.autistichoya.com/2011/11/identity-and-hypocrisy-second-argument.html.

Burgstahler, Sheryl E., ed. 2015. *Universal Design in Higher Education: From Principles to Practice,* 2nd ed. Cambridge, MA: Harvard Education Press.

Burgstahler, Sheryl. 2017. "Equal Access: Universal Design of Instruction." Disabilities, Opportunities, Internetworking, and Technology. https://www.washington.edu/doit/equal-access-universal-design-instruction.

Burgstahler, Sheryl. 2018. "20 Tips for Teaching an Accessible Online Course." Disabilities, Opportunities, Internetworking, and Technology. https://www.washington.edu/doit/20-tips-teaching-accessible-online-course.

Burgstahler, Sheryl, and Rosalie Russo-Gleicher. 2015. "Applying Universal Design to Address the Needs of Postsecondary Students on the Autism Spectrum." *Journal of Postsecondary Education and Disability* 28, no. 2: 199–212. https://eric.ed.gov/?id=EJ1074670.

Cai, Ru Ying, and Amanda L. Richdale. 2016. "Educational Experiences and Needs of Higher Education Students with Autism Spectrum Disorder." *Journal of Autism & Developmental Disorders* 46, no. 1: 31–41. https://doi.org/10.1007/s10803-015-2535-1.

Carter, Toni M., and Priscilla Seaman. 2011. "The Management and Support of Outreach in Academic Libraries." *Reference & User Services Quarterly* 51, no. 2: 163. https://doi.org/10.5860/rusq.51n2.163.

CAST. 2018. "About Universal Design for Learning." Center on Applied Special Technology. http://www.cast.org/our-work/about-udl.html#.W2CVHMInaUm.

Catalano, Amy. 2014. "Improving Distance Education for Students with Special Needs: A Qualitative Study of Students' Experiences with an Online Library Research Course."*Journal of Library & Information Services in Distance Learning* 8, no. 1–2: 17–31. https://doi.org/10.1080/1533290X.2014.902416.

Center for Universal Design. 2008. North Carolina State University. https://projects.ncsu.edu/design/cud/about_ud/about_ud.htm.

Centers for Disease Control and Prevention. n.d. "Autism Spectrum Disorder: Data & Statistics." Accessed September 8, 2017. https://www.cdc.gov/ncbddd/autism/data.html.

Cherney, Kristeen. 2017. "Inclusion for the "Isolated": An Exploration of Writing Tutoring Strategies for Students with ASD." *Praxis* 14, no. 3: 49–55. https://repositories.lib.utexas.edu/handle/2152/61738.

Chickering, Arthur W., and Zelda F. Gamson. 1987. "Seven Principles for Good Practice in Undergraduate Education." Washington, D.C.: American Association for Higher Education. https://eric.ed.gov/?id=ED282491.

Chodock, Ted, and Elizabeth Dolinger. 2009. "Applying Universal Design to Information Literacy: Teaching Students Who Learn Differently at Landmark College." *Reference & User Services Quarterly* 49, no. 1: 24–32. http://dx.doi.org/10.5860/rusq.49n1.24.

Cooke, Nicole A. 2016. *Information Services to Diverse Populations: Developing Culturally Competent Library Professionals.* Santa Barbara, CA: Libraries Unlimited.

Cooper, John, Timothy Heron, and William Heward. 2007. *Applied Behavior Analysis*, 2nd ed. NJ: Pearson.

Cox, Bradley E., Kerry Thompson, Amelia Anderson, Amanda Mintz, Taylor Locks, Lindee Morgan, Jeffrey Edelstein, and Abigail Wolz. 2017. "College Experiences for Students with Autism Spectrum Disorder: Personal Identity, Public Disclosure, and Institutional Support." *Journal of College Student Development* 58, no. 1: 71–87. https://doi.org/10.1353/csd.2017.0004.

Cullen, Jennifer A. 2015. "The Needs of College Students with Autism Spectrum Disorders and Asperger's Syndrome." *Journal of Postsecondary Education and Disability* 28, no. 1: 89–101. https://eric.ed.gov/?id=EJ1066322.

Drake, Sara. 2014. "College Experience of Academically Successful Students with Autism." *Journal of Autism* 1, no. 1: 1–4. https://doi.org/10.7243/2054-992X-1-5.

Dunn, Dana S., and Erin E. Andrews. 2015. "Person-First and Identity-First Language." *American Psychologist* 70, no. 3: 255–264. http://dx.doi .org/10.1037/a0038636.

Elias, Rebecca, Ashley E. Muskett, and Susan W. White. 2017, October 16. "Educator Perspectives on the Postsecondary Transition Difficulties of Students with Autism." *Autism: The International Journal of Research and Practice.* https://doi.org/10.1177/13623613177 26246.

Elias, Rebecca, and Susan W. White. 2018. "Autism Goes to College: Understanding the Needs of a Student Population on the Rise." *Journal of Autism and Developmental Disorders* 48, no. 3: 732–746. https:// doi.org/10.1007/s10803-017-3075-7.

Elwin, Marie, Lena Ek, Lars Kjellin, and Agneta Schröder. 2013. "Too Much or Too Little: Hyper- and Hypo-Reactivity in High-Functioning Autism Spectrum Conditions." *Journal of Intellectual and Developmental Disability* 38, no. 3: 232–241. https://doi.org/10.3109/1366 8250.2013.815694.

Elwin, Marie, Lena Ek, Agneta Schröder, and Lars Kjellin. 2012. "Autobiographical Accounts of Sensing in Asperger Syndrome and High-Functioning Autism." *Archives of Psychiatric Nursing* 26, no. 4: 420–429. https://doi.org/10.1016/j.apnu.2011.10.003.

Fleming, Allison R., Kathleen Marie Oertle, Anthony J. Plotner, and Jonathan G. Hakun. 2017. "Influence of Social Factors on Student Satisfaction among College Students with Disabilities." *Journal of College Student Development* 58, no. 2: 215–228. https://doi.org/10 .1353/csd.2017.0016.

Geller, Lynda L., and Michael Greenberg. 2009. "Managing the Transition Process from High School to College and Beyond: Challenges for Individuals, Families, and Society." *Social Work in Mental Health* 8, no. 1: 92–116. https://doi.org/10.1080/15332980902932466.

Gillespie-Lynch, Kristen, Dennis Bublitz, Annemarie Donachie, Vincent Wong, Patricia J. Brooks, and Joanne Onofrio. 2017, April. "For a Long Time Our Voices Have Been Hushed: Using Student Perspectives to Develop Supports for Neurodiverse College Students." *Frontiers in Psychology* 8. https://doi.org/10.3389/fpsyg.2017.00544.

Glennon, Tara J. 2016. "Survey of College Personnel: Preparedness to Serve Students with Autism Spectrum Disorder." *The American Journal of Occupational Therapy* 70, no. 2: 7002260010. https://doi.org/10 .5014/ajot.2016.017921.

Gobbo, Ken, and Solvegi Shmulsky. 2012. "Classroom Needs of Community College Students with Asperger's Disorder and Autism Spectrum Disorders." *Community College Journal of Research and Practice* 36, no. 1: 40–46. https://eric.ed.gov/?id=EJ952539.

Gobbo, Ken, and Solvegi Shmulsky. 2014. "Faculty Experience with College Students with Autism Spectrum Disorders." *Focus on Autism and Other Developmental Disabilities* 29, no. 1: 13–22. https://doi.org/10.1177/1088357613504989.

Gravel, Jenna W., Laura A. Edwards, Christopher J. Buttimer, and David H. Rose. 2015. "Universal Design for Learning in Postsecondary Education: Reflections on Principles and Their Application." In *Universal Design in Higher Education: From Principles to Practice,* 2nd ed., ed. Sheryl E. Burgstahler. Cambridge, MA: Harvard Education Press.

Hagner, David, and Bernard F. Cooney. 2005. "'I Do That for Everybody': Supervising Employees with Autism." *Focus on Autism and Other Developmental Disabilities* 20, no. 2: 91–97. https://doi.org/10.1177/10883576050200020501.

Hendricks, Dawn. 2010. "Employment and Adults with Autism Spectrum Disorders: Challenges and Strategies for Success." *Journal of Vocational Rehabilitation* 32, no. 2: 125–134. https://doi.org/10.3233/JVR-2010-0502.

Hendrickson, Jo M., Suzanne Woods-Groves, Derek B. Rodgers, and Shawn Datchuk. 2017. "Perceptions of Students with Autism and Their Parents: The College Experience." *Education & Treatment of Children* 40, no. 4: 571–596. https://doi.org//10.1353/etc.2017.0025.

Hendrickx, Sarah. 2010. *The Adolescent and Adult Neuro-Diversity Handbook: Asperger Syndrome, ADHD, Dyslexia, Dyspraxia, and Related Conditions.* Philadelphia: Jessica Kingsley.

Hensel, Wendy. 2017. "People with Autism Spectrum Disorder in the Workplace: An Expanding Legal Frontier." *Harvard Civil Rights—Civil Liberties Law Review* 52, no. 1: 73–102. http://harvardcrcl.org/wp-content/uploads/2017/02/Hensel.pdf.

Hernon, Peter, and Philip Calvert, eds. 2006. *Improving the Quality of Library Services for Students with Disabilities.* Westport, CT: Libraries Unlimited.

Highee, Jeanne L. 2015. "The Faculty Perspective. Implementation of Universal Design in a First-Year Classroom." In *Universal Design in*

Higher Education: From Principles to Practice, 2nd ed., ed. Sheryl E. Burgstahler. Cambridge, MA: Harvard Education Press.

Hill, Elisabeth L. 2004. "Executive Dysfunction in Autism." *Trends in Cognitive Sciences* 8, no. 1: 26–32. https://doi.org/10.1016/j.tics.2003.11.003.

Hillier, Ashleigh, Heather Campbell, and Karen Mastriani. 2007. "Two-Year Evaluation of a Vocational Support Program for Adults on the Autism Spectrum." *Career Development for Exceptional Individuals* 30, no. 1: 35–47. https://doi.org/10.1177/08857288070300010501.

Hillier, Ashleigh, Jody Goldstein, Deirdra Murphy, Rhoda Trietsch, Jacqueline Keeves, Eva Mendes, and Alexa Queenan. 2017. "Supporting University Students with Autism Spectrum Disorder." *Autism* 22, no. 1: 20–28. https://doi.org/10.1177/1362361317699584.

Horder, Jamie, C. Ellie Wilson, M. Andreina Mendez, and Declan G. Murphy. 2014. "Autistic Traits and Abnormal Sensory Experiences in Adults." *Journal of Autism and Developmental Disorders* 44, no. 6: 1461–1469. https://doi.org/10.1007/s10803-013-2012-7.

Howlin, Patricia, Jennifer Alcock, and Catherine Burkin. 2005. "An 8 Year Follow-Up of a Specialist Supported Employment Service for High-Ability Adults with Autism or Asperger Syndrome." *Autism: The International Journal of Research & Practice* 9, no 5: 533–549. https://doi.org/10.1177/1362361305057871.

Izzo, Margaretha, and Vreeburg Bauer. 2015. "Universal Design for Learning: Enhancing Achievement and Employment of STEM Students with Disabilities." *Universal Access in the Information Society* 14, no. 1: 17–27. https://doi.org/10.1007/s10209-013-0332-1.

Jackson, Lynn, Mary Lou Duffy, Michael Brady, and Jazarae McCormick. 2018. "Effects of Learning Strategy Training on the Writing Performance of College Students with Asperger's Syndrome." *Journal of Autism and Developmental Disorders* 48, no. 3: 708–721. https://doi.org/10.1007/s10803-017-3170-9.

Jackson, Scott L. J., Logan Hart, Jane Thierfeld Brown, and Fred R. Volkmar. 2018. "Brief Report: Self-Reported Academic, Social, and Mental Health Experiences of Post-Secondary Students with Autism Spectrum Disorder." *Journal of Autism and Developmental Disorders* 48, no. 3: 643–650. https://doi.org/10.1007/s10803-017-3315-x.

Kanakri, Shireen M., Mardelle Shepley, James W. Varni, and Louis G. Tassinary. 2017. "Noise and Autism Spectrum Disorder in Children:

An Exploratory Survey." *Research in Developmental Disabilities* 63: 85–94. https://doi.org/10.1016/j.ridd.2017.02.004.

Kapp, Steven K., Kristen Gillespie-Lynch, Lauren E. Sherman, and Ted Hutman. 2013. "Deficit, Difference, or Both? Autism and Neurodiversity." *Developmental Psychology* 49, no. 1: 59–71. https://doi.org/10.1037/a0028353.

Kenny, Lorcan, Caroline Hattersley, Bonnie Molins, Carole Buckley, Carol Povey, and Elizabeth Pellicano. 2016. "Which Terms Should Be Used to Describe Autism? Perspectives from the UK Autism Community." *Autism: The International Journal of Research and Practice* 20, no. 4: 442–462. https://doi.org/10.1177/1362361315588200.

Kinnaer, Marijke, Stijn Baumers, and Ann Heylighen. 2016. "Autism-Friendly Architecture from the Outside in and the Inside out: An Explorative Study Based on Autobiographies of Autistic People." *Journal of Housing and the Built Environment* 31, no. 2: 179–195. https://doi.org/10.1007/s10901-015-9451-8.

Kirchner, Jennifer, and Isabel Dziobek. 2014. "Toward the Successful Employment of Adults with Autism: A First Analysis of Special Interests and Factors Deemed Important for Vocational Performance." *Scandinavian Journal of Child and Adolescent Psychiatry and Psychology* 2, no. 2: 77–85. https://doi.org/10.21307/sjcapp-2014-011.

Kirchner, Jennifer, Willibald Ruch, and Isabel Dziobek. 2016. "Brief Report: Character Strengths in Adults with Autism Spectrum Disorder without Intellectual Impairment." *Journal of Autism and Developmental Disorders* 46, no. 10: 3330–3337. https://doi.org/10.1007/s10803-016-2865-7.

Knott, Fiona, and Angela Taylor. 2014. "Life at University with Asperger Syndrome: A Comparison of Student and Staff Perspectives." *International Journal of Inclusive Education* 18, no. 4: 411–426. https://doi.org/10.1080/13603116.2013.781236.

Kuder, S., and Amy Accardo. 2017. "What Works for College Students with Autism Spectrum Disorder." *Journal of Autism and Developmental Disorders* 48, no. 3: 722–731. https://doi.org/10.1007/s10803-017-3434-4.

Kushki, Azadeh, Tom Chau, and Evdokia Anagnostou. 2011. "Handwriting Difficulties in Children with Autism Spectrum Disorders: A Scoping Review." *Journal of Autism and Developmental Disorders* 41, no. 12: 1706–1716. https://doi.org/10.1007/s10803-011-1206-0.

Landon, Jason, Daniel Shepherd, and Veema Lodhia. 2016. "A Qualitative Study of Noise Sensitivity in Adults with Autism Spectrum Disorder." *Research in Autism Spectrum Disorders* 32: 43–52. https://doi.org/10.1016/j.rasd.2016.08.005.

Lawrence, Emily. 2013. "Loud Hands in the Library: Neurodiversity in LIS Theory & Practice." *Progressive Librarian* 41: 98–109. http://www.progressivelibrariansguild.org/PL/PL41/098.pdf.

Leekam, Susan, Carmen Nieto, Sarah Libby, Lorna Wing, and Judith Gould. 2007. "Describing the Sensory Abnormalities of Children and Adults with Autism." *Journal of Autism and Developmental Disorders* 37, no. 5: 894–910. https://doi.org/10.1007/s10803-006-0218-7.

LeGary, Robert A., Jr. 2017. "College Students with Autism Spectrum Disorder: Perceptions of Social Supports That Buffer College-Related Stress and Facilitate Academic Success." *Journal of Postsecondary Education and Disability* 30, no. 3: 251–268. https://eric.ed.gov/?id=EJ1163965.

Longtin, Susan E. 2014. "Using the College Infrastructure to Support Students on the Autism Spectrum." *Journal of Postsecondary Education and Disability* 27, no. 1: 63–72. https://eric.ed.gov/?id=EJ1029568.

Lorenz, Timo, and Kathrin Heinitz. 2014. "Aspergers—Different, Not Less: Occupational Strengths and Job Interests of Individuals with Asperger's Syndrome." *PLoS One* 9, no. 6: 1–8. https://doi.org/10.1371/journal.pone.0100358.

Lyons, Viktoria, and Michael Fitzgerald. 2004. "Humor in Autism and Asperger Syndrome." *Journal of Autism and Developmental Disorders* 34, no. 5: 521–531. https://link.springer.com/article/10.1007/s10803-004-2547-8.

Madriaga, Manuel. 2010. "'I Avoid Pubs and the Student Union Like the Plague': Students with Asperger Syndrome and Their Negotiation of University Spaces." *Children's Geographies* 8, no. 1: 23–34. https://doi.org/10.1080/14733280903500166.

Meeks, Lisa, and Elise Geither. 2014a. *Helping Students with Autism Spectrum Disorder Express Their Thoughts and Knowledge in Writing Tips and Exercises for Developing Writing Skills.* London: Jessica Kingsley.

Meeks, Lisa, and Elise Geither. 2014b. "Writing and the Autism Spectrum: Helping Students through the Process." *Good Autism Practice (GAP)* 15, no. 2: 79–83. http://www.ingentaconnect.com/content/bild/gap/2014/00000015/00000002/art00009.

Meyer, Anne, David H. Rose, and David Gordon. 2014. *Universal Design for Learning: Theory and Practice*. Peabody: CAST.

Miller, Fayneese, ed. 2012. *Transforming Learning Environment: Strategies to Shape the Next Generation*. Bingley, UK: Emerald.

Miner, Meg. 2009. "Working within the Spectrum: Employees with Asperger Syndrome in Our Library." *ILA Reporter* 27, no. 4: 16–20. https://www.ila.org/publications/ila-reporter/issue/36/volume-xxvii-issue-4.

Müller, Eve, Adriana Schuler, Barbara A. Burton, and Gregory B. Yates. 2003. "Meeting the Vocational Support Needs of Individuals with Asperger Syndrome and Other Autism Spectrum Disabilities." *Journal of Vocational Rehabilitation* 18, no. 3: 163–175. EBSCOhost.

Nasamran, Amy N., Sara E. Witmer, and James E. Los. 2017. "Exploring Predictors of Postsecondary Outcomes for Students with Autism Spectrum Disorder." *Education and Training in Autism and Developmental Disabilities* 52, no. 4: 343–356. https://eric.ed.gov/?id=EJ1160232.

National Autism Center. 2009. *Findings and Conclusions: National Standards Project, Phase 1*. Accessed May 23, 2018. http://www.nationalautismcenter.org/national-standards-project.

National Autism Center. 2015. *Findings and Conclusions: National Standards Project, Phase 2*. Accessed May 23, 2018. http://www.nationalautismcenter.org/national-standards-project.

O'Keeffe, Patrick. 2013. "A Sense of Belonging: Improving Student Retention." *College Student Journal* 47, no. 4: 605–613. https://eric.ed.gov/?id=EJ1029294.

Organization for Autism Research. 2012. "Understanding Autism: An Employer's Guide." Accessed June 10. https://researchautism.org/resources/understanding-autism-an-employers-guide.

Otto-Meyer, Sebastian, Jennifer Krizman, Travis White-Schwoch, and Nina Kraus. 2018. "Children with Autism Spectrum Disorder Have Unstable Neural Responses to Sound." *Experimental Brain Research* 236, no. 3: 733–743. https://doi.org/10.1007/s00221-017-5164-4.

Parker, Holly Buckland. 2012. "Learning Starts with Design: Using Universal Design for Learning (UDL) in Higher Education Course Redesign." In *Transforming Learning Environment: Strategies to Shape the Next Generation*, ed. Fayneese Miller. Bingley, UK: Emerald.

Parr, Alissa D., and Samuel T. Hunter. 2014. "Enhancing Work Outcomes of Employees with Autism Spectrum Disorder through Leadership:

Leadership for Employees with Autism Spectrum Disorder." *Autism: The International Journal of Research and Practice* 18, no. 5: 545–554. https://doi.org/10.1177/1362361313483020.

Plavnick, Joshua, and Kara Hume. 2014. "Observational Learning by Individuals with Autism: A Review of Teaching Strategies." *Autism: The International Journal of Research and Practice* 18, no. 4: 458–466. https://doi.org/10.1177/1362361312474373.

Polger, Mark Aaron, and Scott Sheidlower. 2017. *Engaging Diverse Learners: Teaching Strategies for Academic Librarians.* Santa Barbara, CA: Libraries Unlimited.

Remy, Charlie, and Priscilla Seaman. 2014. "Evolving from Disability to Diversity: How to Better Serve High-Functioning Autistic Students." *Reference & User Services Quarterly* 54, no. 1: 24–28. https://journals.ala.org/rusq/article/download/3968/4454.

Richardson, John T. E. 2017. "Academic Attainment in Students with Autism Spectrum Disorders in Distance Education." *Open Learning* 32, no. 1: 81–91. https://doi.org/10.1080/02680513.2016.1272446.

Robertson, Ashley E., and David R. Simmons. 2013. "The Relationship between Sensory Sensitivity and Autistic Traits in the General Population." *Journal of Autism and Developmental Disorders* 43, no. 4: 775–784. https://doi.org/10.1007/s10803-012-1608-7.

Robertson, Scott M., and Ari D. Ne'eman. 2008. "Autistic Acceptance, the College Campus, and Technology: Growth of Neurodiversity in Society and Academia." *Disability Studies Quarterly* 28, no. 4. https://doi.org/10.18061/dsq.v28i4.146.

Robledo, Jodi, Anne M. Donnellan, and Karen Strandt-Conroy. 2012. "An Exploration of Sensory and Movement Differences from the Perspective of Individuals with Autism." *Frontiers in Integrative Neuroscience* 6: article 107. https://doi.org/10.3389/fnint.2012.00107.

Roux, Anne M., Paul T. Shattuck, Benjamin P. Cooper, Kristy A. Anderson, Mary Wagner, and Sarah C. Narendorf. 2013. "Postsecondary Employment Experiences among Young Adults with an Autism Spectrum Disorder." *Journal of the American Academy of Child & Adolescent Psychiatry* 52, no. 9: 931–939. https://doi.org/10.1016/j.jaac.2013.05.019.

Salamon, Anaïs. 2016. "Benefits and Challenges of Outreach in Academic Libraries: A Case Study at the McGill Islamic Studies Library." *MELA Notes* 89: 1–14. https://www.jstor.org/stable/44176057.

Samson, Andrea C., and Yovanni Antonelli. 2013. "Humor as Character Strength and Its Relation to Life Satisfaction and Happiness in Autism Spectrum Disorders." *Humor: International Journal of Humor Research* 26, no. 3: 477–491. https://doi.org/10.1515/humor-2013-0031.

Sarrett, Jennifer. 2017. "Autism and Accommodations in Higher Education: Insights from the Autism Community." *Journal of Autism and Developmental Disorders* 48, no. 3: 679–693. https://doi.org/10.1007/s10803-017-3353-4.

Satterfield, Debra, Christopher Lepage, and Nora Ladjahasan. 2015. "Preferences for Online Course Delivery Methods in Higher Education for Students with Autism Spectrum Disorders." *Procedia Manufacturing* 3: 3651–3656. https://doi.org/10.1016/j.promfg.2015.07.758.

Sayman, Donna M. 2015. "I Still Need My Security Teddy Bear: Experiences of an Individual with Autism Spectrum Disorder in Higher Education." *Learning Assistance Review* 20, no. 1: 77–98. https://eric.ed.gov/?id=EJ1058012.

Schall, Carol, Paul Wehman, and Staci Carr. 2014. "Transition from High School to Adulthood for Adolescents and Young Adults with Autism Spectrum Disorders." In *Adolescents and Adults with Autism Spectrum Disorders,* ed. Fred R. Volkmar, Brian Reichow, and James C. McPartland. New York: Springer.

Schindler, Victoria, Abigail Cajiga, Rae Aaronson, and Lorena Salas. 2015. "The Experience of Transition to College for Students Diagnosed with Asperger's Disorder." *Open Journal of Occupational Therapy* 3, no. 1: 1–17. https://scholarworks.wmich.edu/ojot/vol3/iss1/2.

Schriber, Roberta A., Richard W. Robins, and Marjorie Solomon. 2014. "Personality and Self-Insight in Individuals with Autism Spectrum Disorder." *Journal of Personality and Social Psychology* 106, no. 1: 112–130. https://doi.org/10.1037/a0034950.

Scott, Sally S., Joan M. McGuire, and Stan F. Shaw. 2003. "Universal Design for Instruction—A New Paradigm for Adult Instruction in Postsecondary Education." *Remedial and Special Education* 24, no. 6: 369–79. https://doi.org/10.1177/07419325030240060801.

Shattuck, Paul T., Sarah Carter Narendorf, Benjamin Cooper, Paul R. Sterzing, Mary Wagner, and Julie Lounds Taylor. 2012. "Postsecondary Education and Employment among Youth with an Autism Spectrum Disorder." *Pediatrics* 129, no. 6. https://doi.org/10.1542/peds.2011-2864.

Shaw, Robert A. 2011. "Employing Universal Design for Instruction." *New Directions for Student Services*, no. 134: 21–33. https://doi.org/10.1002/ss.392.

Shmulsky, Solvegi, Ken Gobbo, Andy T. Donahue, and Manju Banerjee. 2017. "College Students Who Have ASD: Factors Related to First Year Performance." *Journal of Postsecondary Education and Disability* 30, no. 4: 373–382. https://eric.ed.gov/?id=EJ1172785.

Sinclair, Jim. 1999. "Why I Dislike Person First Language." Accessed September 26, 2017. http://web.archive.org/web/20090210190652/http://web.syr.edu/~jisincla/person_first.htm.

Small, Ruth V., William N. Myhill, and Lydia Herring-Harrington. 2015. "Developing Accessible Libraries and Inclusive Librarians in the 21st Century: Examples from Practice." *Advances in Librarianship* 40: 73–88. https://doi.org/10.1108/S0065-283020150000040013.

Smith, Heather. 2017. "Designing with Autism in Mind: CMU Student's Proposal Sparks Discussions to Improve Signage for People with ASD." *Central Michigan University News.* https://www.cmich.edu/news/article/Pages/InteriorDesignsupportsASD.aspx.

Smith, Richard S., and Jonathan Sharp. 2013. "Fascination and Isolation: A Grounded Theory Exploration of Unusual Sensory Experiences in Adults with Asperger Syndrome." *Journal of Autism and Developmental Disorders* 43, no. 4: 891–910. https://doi.org/10.1007/s10803-012-1633-6.

Sosnowy, Collette, Chloe Silverman, and Paul Shattuck. 2017, October 11. "Parents' and Young Adults' Perspectives on Transition Outcomes for Young Adults with Autism." *Autism: The International Journal of Research and Practice.* https://doi.org/10.1177/1362361317699585.

South, Mikle, Sally Ozonoff, and William M. McMahon. 2005. "Repetitive Behavior Profiles in Asperger Syndrome and High-Functioning Autism." *Journal of Autism and Developmental Disorders* 35, no. 2: 145–158. https://doi.org/10.1007/s10803-004-1992-8.

Staines, Gail M. 2012. *Universal Design: A Practical Guide to Creating and Recreating Interiors of Academic Libraries for Teaching, Learning, and Research.* Oxford, UK: Chandos.

Stiegler, Ln, and R. Davis. 2010. "Understanding Sound Sensitivity in Individuals with Autism Spectrum Disorders." *Focus on Autism and Other Developmental Disabilities.* 25, no. 2: 67–75. https://doi.org/10.1177/1088357610364530.

Strub, Maurini R., and Louann Stewart. 2010. "Case Study: Shelving and the Autistic Employee." *Journal of Access Services* 7, no. 4: 262–268. https://doi.org/10.1080/15367967.2010.508369.

Taylor, Julie, and Marsha Seltzer. 2010. "Employment and Post-Secondary Educational Activities for Young Adults with Autism Spectrum Disorders during the Transition to Adulthood." *Journal of Autism & Developmental Disorders* 41, no. 5: 566–574. https://doi.org/10.1007/s10803-010-1070-3.

Thompson, Craig, Sven Bolte, Torbjorn Falkmer, and Sonya Girdler. 2018. "To Be Understood: Transitioning to Adult Life for People with Autism Spectrum Disorder." *PLoS ONE* 13, no. 3. https://doi.org/10.1371/journal.pone.0194758.

Tomlinson, Elizabeth, and Newman, Sara. 2017. "Valuing Writers from a Neurodiversity Perspective: Integrating New Research on Autism Spectrum Disorder into Composition Pedagogy." *Composition Studies* 45, no. 2: 91–112. https://eric.ed.gov/?id=EJ1159661.

Tops, Wim, An Van Den Bergh, Ilse Noens, and Dieter Baeyens. 2017. "A Multi-Method Assessment of Study Strategies in Higher Education Students with an Autism Spectrum Disorder." *Learning and Individual Differences* 59: 141–148. https://doi.org/10.1016/j.lindif.2017.09.003.

UDI Online Project. 2009. "Examples of UDI in Online and Blended Courses." Center on Postsecondary Education and Disability, University of Connecticut, Storrs. http://udi.uconn.edu/index.php?q=content/examples-udi-online-and-blended-courses.

United States Department of Education, National Center for Education Statistics. 2016. *Digest of Education Statistics, 2015.* https://nces.ed.gov/fastfacts/display.asp?id=60.

Van Hees, Valérie, Tinneke Moyson, and Herbert Roeyers. 2015. "Higher Education Experiences of Students with Autism Spectrum Disorder: Challenges, Benefits and Support Needs." *Journal of Autism & Developmental Disorders* 45, no. 6: 1673–1688. https://doi.org/10.1007/s10803-014-2324-2.

Webb, Katy Kavanagh, and Jeanne Hoover. 2015. "Universal Design for Learning (UDL) in the Academic Library: A Methodology for Mapping Multiple Means of Representation in Library Tutorials." *College & Research Libraries* 76, no. 4: 537–553. https://eric.ed.gov/?id=EJ1061467.

White, Susan W., Rebecca Elias, Nicole N. Capriola-Hall, Isaac C. Smith, Caitlin M. Conner, Susan B. Asselin, Patricia Howlin, Elizabeth E. Getzel, and Carla A. Mazefsky. 2017. "Development of a College Transition and Support Program for Students with Autism Spectrum Disorder." *Journal of Autism and Developmental Disorders* 47, no. 10: 3072–3078. https://doi.org/10.1007/s10803-017-3236-8

White, Susan W., Thomas H. Ollendick, and Bethany C. Bray. 2011. "College Students on the Autism Spectrum." *Autism* 15, no. 6: 683–701. https://doi.org/10.1177/1362361310393363.

Wolf, Lorraine E., Jane Thierfeld Brown, and G. Ruth Kukiela Bork. 2009. *Students with Asperger Syndrome: A Guide for College Personnel.* Shawnee Mission, KS: Autism Asperger.

Zager, Dianne, and Carol S. Alpern. 2010. "College-Based Inclusion Programming for Transition-Age Students with Autism." *Focus on Autism and Other Developmental Disabilities* 25, no. 3: 151–157. https://doi.org/10.1177/1088357610371331.

Zager, Dianne, Carol Alpern, Barbara McKeon, Susan Maxam, and Janet Mulvey. 2013. *Educating College Students with Autism Spectrum Disorders.* New York: Routledge.

Zhong, Ying. 2012. "Universal Design for Learning (UDL) in Library Instruction." *College & Undergraduate Libraries* 19, no. 1: 33–45. https://doi.org/10.1080/10691316.2012.652549.

Index

About the Authors

Rachel M. McMullin is an associate professor and humanities/information literacy librarian at West Chester University of Pennsylvania. She works closely with students as a reference and instruction librarian who teaches more than 100 library information literacy sessions a year.

Kerry R. Walton is an assistant professor and electronic resources librarian at West Chester University of Pennsylvania, where she provides reference services, instruction, and support for electronic resources to students, faculty, and staff. Prior to working at West Chester, Kerry provided reference services and instruction at branch campuses for Delaware County Community College, where she worked closely with diverse student populations.